HOW TO MASTER JAPANESE

A Roadmap to Fluent, Functional, Marketable Japanese

By Shane Jones

Published by NJM Publishing

FORWARD

Most beginning learners of Japanese embark on their journey toward mastery of the language with excitement, optimism, and perhaps a bit of trepidation at the unknown path ahead. They envision the day when they will soon be conversing fluently with friends in Japanese, reading manga and novels, watching movies and anime and consuming other media in the original language, and even living in Japan and working in a career in which they use Japanese on an everyday basis in the workplace.

Then day one of the first day of Japanese 101 arrives, and the learner is hit with a cold, sobering realization: learning Japanese is *hard*, and the journey ahead will be a long, arduous one in which only the strong, studious, prepared and persistent will survive.

In order to survive any long journey and arrive surely at one's destination, a reliable roadmap is essential. *How to Master Japanese* is the story of my own long, arduous struggle to master Japanese. It is the story of many false starts and early failures and many frustrations along the way. It is a cautionary tale of the many pitfalls to avoid. But it is also a story of persistence and overcoming of obstacles, and the eventual rewards that come from continuing to climb, even after being knocked down repeatedly, to eventually reach the promised land of mastery of the Japanese language, and with it, the key to Japanese culture and many incredible relationships and experiences with even career rewards to be gained as a result.

I wrote *How to Master Japanese* to provide aspiring learners with a roadmap to their own successful journey toward Japanese mastery. This is NOT your run-of-the-mill Japanese textbook. You won't learn Japanese grammar, hiragana, katakana, or kanji by reading this book. But follow along with me and I will show you how I went from a 24-year-old Midwesterner who couldn't speak a word of Japanese to someone who quickly evolved into a highly fluent speaker and reader of Japanese and, within just a few years of beginning the study of Japanese, was and still is today teaching, translating, interpreting, speaking and using the Japanese language on a daily basis at a high level of fluency in a professional capacity.

You see, there is no shortage of excellent resources for learning the Japanese language. There are countless high-quality textbooks and kanji books, online learning tools and even apps, as well as many fine institutional classroom programs all over the world. If simply having access to good study material or a learning environment were the key to language learning success, anyone today with an Internet connection or a good textbook would become a successful learner. However, without the proper insight and understanding of what it *really* takes to master Japanese, the reality is that most aspiring Japanese learners ultimately fail in their quest to master the language or even gain a basic level of fluency.

In *How to Master Japanese*, I will take you with me on my journey from my initial aspirations and motivation to learn Japanese, to my early failures to complete even Japanese 101 before finally gaining a measure of success in the classroom, to struggling with and eventually conquering kanji and gaining the ability to read Japanese at an advanced level, to struggling to live and work in Japan and fit into its oftentimes hard-to-crack culture and eventually succeeding at finding a level of comfort and acceptance and forming many lasting relationships with Japanese counterparts, to becoming a professional Japanese translator and interpreter and Japanese language instructor, and continuing to maintain and even improve my Japanese years after moving back home in my life after Japan.

As you read, a full picture of what it really takes to succeed at Japanese, both inside the classroom and beyond, in order to attain a true functional proficiency in the language will emerge. Equally as important, you will learn how to negotiate the many unique nuances of Japanese culture, as well as avoid the many pitfalls and detours in the learning process that can result in years, if not an entire lifetime, of lost time and frustrated effort in attempting to learn the Japanese language and understand the complicated intricacies of Japanese culture.

Embarking on the journey toward mastery of the Japanese language is by far the most challenging and rewarding thing I have ever done in my life. It is a journey that is still and will forever be in progress, and one that has bestowed upon me rewards, in the form of friendships, experiences, career fulfillment and even monetary gain, beyond my wildest expectations.

I wish you the very best of success on your own journey toward mastery of the Japanese language and discovery of the Japanese culture, and sincerely hope that this book will help you realize your own Japanese aspirations. If a young, not-so-bright Midwestern adult with no special aptitude for language learning like me can master Japanese, than so can you!

TABLE OF CONTENTS

INTRODUCTION

First, a word about what it means to "master" Japanese. What does it really mean to "master" Japanese, or any language for that matter? Does mastering Japanese imply knowledge of every vocabulary word, every element of grammar, and every single kanji? Does it mean speaking, reading, writing and comprehending the language at a level equivalent to a native speaker? Since few if any of us have mastered every single nuance of our own native language, clearly it is not possible to master every single nuance of a foreign language, let alone Japanese. If that is the case, then what are we really talking about when it comes to "mastering" a foreign language?

The Merriam-Webster dictionary defines "mastery" as follows:

"Knowledge and skill that allows you to do, use,
or understand something very well."

As it relates to Japanese, when I speak of mastery in this book, I simply mean gaining a sufficient grasp of the language at some satisfactory functional level that enables you to use the Japanese language, and by doing so directly access the Japanese culture, for whatever purpose you may have, whether that be using your Japanese for your business or career, making and communicating with Japanese friends, living in Japan, traveling to Japan, studying in Japan, consuming Japanese media, such as novels, manga and anime, Japanese film or TV, in the original language, or perhaps even forming and maintaining a romantic relationship with a Japanese-speaking partner.

When it comes to Japanese, mastering the language also means mastering the many unique nuances and social conventions of Japanese culture, so that you not only use the language fluently, but in a culturally and socially appropriate manner as well, for when it comes to Japanese, the language and the cultural context in which it is used are intimately intertwined.

In my own case, mastering Japanese has meant gaining verbal fluency in the language so that I can carry on conversations in Japanese with Japanese friends and acquaintances, conduct business in Japanese with Japanese clients and associates, and negotiate my way through Japanese culture and in Japanese-speaking social circles without any reliance on English whatsoever.

It has meant gaining enough competence with the written language so that I can read Japanese newspapers, magazines, websites, novels, manga, and read and write emails, letters and other correspondences. It has meant acquiring sufficient listening comprehension so that I can watch Japanese film and TV, including news and variety shows, Japanese dramas and Japanese anime, without any reliance on English subtitles.

Mastering Japanese has meant acquiring a sufficient grasp of the Japanese language so that I have the ability to translate it and interpret and even teach it on a professional level, enabling me to enjoy using the language on a daily basis in my work and earn a generous income in an interesting and fulfilling manner through use of the language.

Finally, mastering Japanese has meant gaining enough proficiency in the language so that through it, I have acquired the "key" to the culture that enables me to live in Japan, travel throughout Japan, communicate in Japanese, and otherwise experience Japanese culture at a level of depth simply not available to those who have either not yet embarked on this journey, or who are only now just beginning to scratch the surface.

I wrote How to Master Japanese as both a memoir of my own journey and struggles to master the language, and as a guide that I sincerely hope will inspire you on your own journey toward mastery of Japanese and, through a high-level grasp of the language, enable you to acquire the same essential "key" to the culture, so that you too may gain and enjoy the "knowledge and skill that allows you to do, use, or understand Japanese very well!"

PART 1:

The Journey toward Mastery Begins with a Single Step

Finding Your Motivation to Learn

When people I encounter overhear me speaking fluent Japanese or learn that I translate and teach Japanese for a living, they almost always ask me (usually while also remarking at how hopeless they are at learning foreign languages!) how I managed to gain such a high level of proficiency in Japanese. I always tell them this:

Motivation and persistence, not natural talent, are the most essential keys to foreign language learning success.

You see, although it is certainly not my intention at the very outset of this book to dissuade you from attempting to master the Japanese language, I can say from decades of experience and observation that the process of learning a foreign language is a difficult one that requires a long-term commitment of time and effort and, above all, persistence. Without sufficient motivation, the reality is that even the most naturally talented aspiring learners of Japanese simply give up at some point in the process in the face of the difficulty and duration of the task. Therefore, when people ask me what the most essential key to mastering a language is, without hesitation I always answer: your motivation to learn!

What is *your* motivation for learning Japanese? Are you a fan of Japanese manga and anime and other pop culture with a desire to consume these media in the original language? Do you have dreams of traveling to and living in Japan someday in order to experience its unique and fascinating culture? Are you motivated to learn Japanese as a way of furthering your business or career? Do you wish to make and converse with Japanese friends? Do you harbor a secret yearning to meet your dream Japanese romantic partner?

As you embark on this language learning journey, take a moment to identify your own motivation, so that you can define for yourself *why* you want to learn Japanese. The ability to recall and reaffirm your underlying motivation will prove useful down the line to help you keep moving forward when you initially encounter difficulty and frustration, which you most certainly will at some point (probably quite early on!) in your language learning journey.

Today, most fresh Japanese language learners I encounter initially become acquainted with the language through Japanese pop culture, such as manga, anime and JPOP. However, back when I first began learning Japanese, Japanese pop culture had not yet entered the mainstream. Instead, Japan was still viewed as an emerging global economic powerhouse, and many aspiring learners saw gaining competency in Japanese as a means of advancing one's business or career.

My own earliest exposure to Japanese culture came courtesy of the local Japanese restaurant that my mom and dad, both sushi lovers even before sushi entered the American mainstream, took me to on a regular basis as a young child. Although sushi was beyond my palate at that age, I can still remember the delicately prepared tempura that I always ordered, arranged artfully in a bamboo basket. I can remember being soothed by the tranquil music of the *shakuhachi* (a Japanese wooden flute) and *koto* (a Japanese stringed instrument) that played in the background, the refined lacquer tableware, and even the Japanese waitresses clad in colorful kimonos who seemed to radiate an almost ethereal serenity and politeness that I had never encountered in American culture.

By the time I graduated high school I had also graduated to eating sushi, and my friends and I would go out to our favorite sushi spot nearly every weekend. Around this time, I also became absorbed with the study of Zen Buddhist philosophy, which further perked my interest in Japanese culture.

After working various odd jobs for a couple years in order to save up enough money to begin college, I minored in art and developed an interest in Japanese ceramic folk art. It was around this time that I first began to imagine traveling to Japan one day in hopes of apprenticing under a Japanese ceramics master.

This inspiration led me to enroll in my first Japanese class. Up to this point in my life, I had been an indifferent and entirely unsuccessful language learner, and in fact I barely passed two years of required Spanish in high school, which I somehow managed to get through without retaining a single word of the language or the ability to put even a simple sentence together.

It is therefore not surprising that my first attempt at learning Japanese ended quickly in failure. I simply was not prepared for the onslaught of new unfamiliar sounds, endless vocabulary lists or the barrage of hiragana, katakana and kanji memorization and reading assignments. I didn't last more than a week or two in my first class before I dropped out, completely unable to keep pace. I cannot say whether the teacher I had in that first class was a good instructor or not, but it really didn't matter. What I learned firsthand then, and have since observed many times, is that the process of learning a foreign language, much less a difficult one like Japanese, is a much different one than the type of learning that takes place in a typical lecture class. Therefore:

If the Japanese language student is not prepared to process the coursework, even the best teacher and best curriculum in the world will be of no help.

At the time of my first attempt to learn Japanese, I was simply not prepared for nor had any clue how to process this flood of new and unfamiliar information, and therefore was doomed to failure from the outset.

Having failed in my initial quest and convinced I had no capacity to learn the Japanese language, or any language for that matter, I gave up thoughts about traveling to Japan or learning Japanese. However, my association with Japan did not end there.

I continued to study art and draw inspiration from Japanese ceramics. I also took a course in modern Japanese history from an inspiring professor, which further deepened my interest in Japanese culture. However, my family's fortunes changed around this time, and with my own school funds dwindling, I took a break from school that ended up lasting three years in order to help out with my family's business.

Although I'm glad for the experience I gained working in the family business, toward the end of these three years I began to feel stuck in my hometown and started longing to get back to the life I had previously imagined for myself. I once again began to dream of traveling to and living in Japan. I began to recall my fascination with Japan, and started creating ceramic art again. I also developed an interest in Japanese literature (in English of course), devouring books by such famous Japanese authors as Yukio Mishima, Yasunori Kawabata, and Haruki Murakami.

These books, along with my desire to get as far away from my uninspiring Midwestern life as possible, further fueled my imagination and my desire to travel to and experience Japan, and they also perked my desire to attempt to learn the language again. However, still intimidated by the prospect of classroom learning as a result of my initial experience of failure, instead of throwing myself into the deep end again and taking a class I opted instead to cautiously dip my toe in and buy a Japanese language CD in order to study at my own pace.

First Japanese Learning Success

I can still remember the trepidation and excitement I felt putting the CD in my Walkman (I know I'm dating myself here), putting my headphones on, and beginning my first lesson. I remember how excited I was to learn my first basic phrases, such as:

Konnichiwa (Good afternoon; hello)

Hajimemashite (Nice to meet you)

Ogenki desu ka (How are you doing?)

Wakarimasu ka (Do you understand?)

Onamae wa nan desu ka (What is your name?)

Ima nanji desu ka (What time is it now?)

Oyasumi nasai (Good night)

Very basic stuff, I realize, but for me at that time, I was, for the first time in my life, finally learning real Japanese, at my own pace, in a way that I could absorb, and it was a groundbreaking experience. This small success with informal self-study inspired me to make another attempt at learning Japanese in a structured classroom environment.

Looking around town, I found a Japanese 101 course being offered at a nearby community college, which met for four hours per session each Saturday morning. This arrangement worked perfectly for me, and this time I was more motivated and, I believed, better prepared.

Succeeding in Classroom Japanese

Looking back now, although earlier I stated that no teacher can overcome a lack of proper preparation to learn on the part of the student, I also know firsthand how important the influence of a great instructor can be on whether the student ultimately succeeds or fails to learn a language, particularly at the beginning of that student's learning experience.

Even for a prepared and willing learner, the quality of your instructor and learning environment, particularly at the outset, can greatly influence whether you ultimately succeed or fail in learning Japanese

From the day I walked into my first day of this Japanese 101 class, it was as if the stars had finally aligned on my side. My teacher, Peggy-sensei, provided just the right mix of quality instruction and engaging learning environment without making the class too difficult or intimidating, while also making the learning process a whole lot of fun! Somehow, the fact that she was a non-native Japanese who had mastered Japanese at a high level was both inspiring and comforting, which further inspired me and gave me confidence. There were also two Japanese exchange student class volunteers who further lent an air of authenticity to the learning process and made the classroom experience more enjoyable.

This mix of my own renewed motivation meshed perfectly with Peggy-sensei's gentle but enthusiastic teaching style, and whereas I had utterly failed at my previous attempt at learning Japanese, in this class I found myself thriving. Somehow, the process of learning Japanese, which previously had felt like a form of torture, had become transformed, for me, into an exciting journey I couldn't get enough of.

Outside of class, I diligently studied my lessons for the upcoming week on my own. I found myself watching my calendar each week waiting for Saturday to arrive, excited about what the next class would bring.

As the class progressed and I continued to gain confidence in my ability to learn, a new plan began to form in my mind. Having saved up a bit of money and with the family business now stable, I decided that I would go back to school and major in Japanese.

Once I made this decision, somehow everything began to click into place. It turned out that Peggy-sensei had received her Master's degree in Japanese language education from the Ohio State University, which happened to be the school I was planning to attend, and so she arranged for me to visit the OSU campus and sit in on a class.

I did so, became even more excited by the prospect of renewing my studies, and completed the application process with a plan to move to OSU in the summer of 1994. Even better, I learned that OSU had an intensive summer Japanese learning program. In this program, classes met for up to five hours per day, and the program actually crammed the entire first-year curriculum into a single summer quarter. Since I was eager to get started this was even better than I had hoped for! I promptly enrolled.

Since I had completed Japanese 101 at the community college, I tested into Japanese 102. As a result, I had to wait about three weeks into the program until Japanese 102 started, and so I eagerly awaited the start of my class, albeit with nervous anticipation at what lay ahead.

Looking back, these initial small successes, particularly given that fact that I was anything but a naturally talented learner and had previously failed in my first attempts to learning foreign languages, were essential in planting the seeds of belief that maybe, just maybe, I could actually learn Japanese.

Your own initial success or failure at learning Japanese will be highly influenced by your own preparation and motivation to learn. This book will help prepare you for what is to come and hopefully inspire you on your way as well, but particularly for those who have never studied a foreign language or have yet to be successful in doing so and are lacking in confidence, I recommend that you start with baby steps so that you can achieve an initial success in your effort. Doing so will give you the empowering confidence that you can do even more, and your initial success will hopefully excite you and fuel your motivation to keep moving forward.

Surviving Intensive Japanese

If Peggy-sensei's Japanese class was like an infant being introduced to swimming at the gentle hands of a protective mother, the summer intensive program was like being tossed head first into deep cold water and being forced to either sink or swim in a pool of great white sharks.

Intensive does not even begin to describe the frenzied pace of the summer program at OSU. New material came at us so fast and furiously that there was barely time to process it. Moreover, this Japanese class was structured unlike any class in any subject I had ever taken in any subject at any school.

In the OSU Japanese program, Japanese language classes were divided into two types: ACT classes and FACT classes. FACT classes met roughly once for every several ACT classes, and were classes in which the instructor delivered lectures in English on Japanese grammar and usage, and where students could likewise freely ask any questions they had about Japanese in English.

ACT classes, in contrast, met three or four times a day and were based on one strict rule: Japanese only! This Japanese-only rule even applied to the very first day of Japanese 101. Moreover, not only were we not permitted to speak a word of English during these ACT classes, the grade we received was based almost entirely on our ability to actually perform the Japanese that was covered in a particular class. We were given a "daily grade" for each class from 0 to 4 points, with 4 being a perfect score, and points were deducted any time we opened our mouth and made an error in grammar, usage, or pronunciation.

Needless to say, the classroom environment in these ACT classes was extremely intense. We were always under pressure, knowing that our success in the class was dependent upon whether or not we could perform each day.

In order to prepare for an ACT class, we were required to listen to audio tapes (yes, actual tapes, not even CDs at that time much less MP3 files!) that contained the grammar, vocabulary, and sentence patterns for each lesson. In order to properly be prepared to perform in the ACT class and therefore avoid making mistakes and having points deducted, it was necessary to listen to these tapes over and over again, repeating after them out loud, so that we would be fully prepared to perform them properly in the upcoming class.

We also had "core conversations" that began each new chapter, which contained the essential grammatical components and concepts of each chapter's lesson. Our very first task for each new chapter was to memorize the core conversations in their entirety, and then be prepared to literally stand up and act them out in front of the entire class. Of course we were also graded based on our ability to perform these conversations, so it was a little bit like having to master lines of an audition for a new play in which we had to perform the starring role each day, but do so in a foreign language we did not yet speak.

Moreover, whenever we made a mistake in our ACT class, the teacher would always correct us immediately and make us repeat our utterance until we got it right. There was no room to slack off, as poor preparation would ultimately result in a poor grade for the class. Moreover, given the breakneck pace of the intensive program, if a student got behind on just a couple of lessons, in many cases there would be no way to catch back up to the class.

In order to properly prepare for each class and keep up with the frenetic pace of the program, in addition to the five hours of class each day I probably spent an additional 5-6 hours simply studying and practicing my Japanese. It was about as close to full immersion in Japanese as one could possibly get without actually being in Japan.

We had a language lab that was useful for listening to the tapes that were so essential to our progress, and this language lab became my second home as I spent hours there each day listening to the Japanese tapes, desperately trying to process and practice all of the new material.

Once I was home it was more of the same. More hours each night listening to copies of the tapes on my Walkman and endlessly repeating the material out loud. If I wanted to survive in this class, there was no alternative to do anything else.

It was intensive. It was exhausting. It was highly challenging. And I loved it! Actually, I can look back now and say that I loved it, but the reality of the time was one of considerable struggle and frustration. Although I was fully committed to learning the Japanese language, I was by no means a "natural" learner and the process, from beginning to end, was anything but easy. I can remember falling asleep over my books more than once, and I'm not ashamed to admit that I cried on more than one occasion with frustration over my inability to grasp the material.

Nonetheless, I intuitively recognized that there was something uniquely special about this program, so I decided to trust the curriculum and my instructors and commit to the process. At the time I enrolled in the OSU program, I was not aware that it offered such a unique approach to Japanese language learning. Looking back, I cannot help thinking how lucky I was to have stumbled into this program. I often wonder whether I would have ultimately succeeded as a Japanese language learner without this intensely challenging but obviously very-well-conceived learning environment. Although my motivation to learn Japanese by that time was very high, I have since realized that in most cases, successful classroom language learning is the product of the combination of excellent instruction on the part of the teacher, a well-structured curriculum, and sincere effort on the part of the student. If any of these components are lacking, so too will be the end product.

Successful classroom language learning is the product of the combination of excellent instruction on the part of the teacher, a well-structured curriculum and learning environment, and sincere effort on the part of the student. If any of these components are lacking, so too will be the end product.

As the summer intensive Japanese program progressed, the pace never subsided and learning the language never got any easier. In fact, most of the time I felt as though I was barely processing the new material and was forgetting more Japanese than I was learning. I can remember one particular class in which our head instructor, Noda-sensei, dismissed us early in disgust after a particularly brutal session in which no one was able to even put a simple coherent sentence together.

What I did not realize at the time is that this sequence of language input, short-term memorization, forgetfulness, and constant struggle to process, comprehend and produce the language together with the ongoing battle with frustration is all part of the learning process, particularly in the early learning stages.

Even though I felt like I wanted to give up many times, I stuck with the program. The truth is, I really had no choice. I had burned my bridges and placed myself in a situation where I was either going to sink or swim.

Upon reflection, I believe that the situation I placed myself in having no way to retreat was essential to my success as a Japanese language learner. If I had approached Japanese language learning simply as something I was doing as a hobby at my own convenience, I almost certainly would have thrown in the towel when the going got tough. Indeed, throughout my four years' worth of undergraduate classroom language instruction, as well as my years teaching, I witnessed many a classmate start out strong but eventually drop out along the way, unable to keep up the pace or unwilling to cope with the difficulty.

During this process, I learned that by far the most important attribute of a successful language learner is not intellect, but rather, persistence. Learning a language *is* extremely challenging, and many times you will feel overwhelmed, as I did, and be tempted to give up. However, I can promise you that if you just persist with your learning and stay the course, eventually you *will* gain the ability to speak, read and write Japanese at a high level! The ones that fail to do so fail simply because they throw in the towel and give up at some point along the way.

By far the most important attribute of a successful Japanese language learner is persistence! Provided you just persist with your learning and stay the course, eventually you will gain the ability to speak, read and write Japanese at a high level!

The summer of learning dragged on and by the end of the intensive session I was thoroughly exhausted, but I managed to get through both 102 and 103 with "A" grades. The end of the summer quarter culminated in a language festival that included an interpretation contest against the Chinese language students who were going through a similar program in Chinese. I remember how exciting it was to actually be able to interpret Japanese. I remember being able to communicate with my teachers in simple Japanese and thank them for teaching me over the course of the summer quarter.

Although happy for a chance to finally rest and recharge my batteries, there was a part of me that was sad that the summer program was coming to an end. I realized that through the course of this program, I had been challenged in a way I'd never in my life been challenged before to do something I wasn't at all sure I could

16

do. The intensively challenging nature of this program required me to dig deeper into myself than ever before, and I was surprised to find that, with the proper motivation and guidance, I was more capable of responding and rising up to the challenge than I would have ever imagined prior to beginning the program.

This knowledge that I had survived such an intensive program actually did more than simply accelerate my Japanese language acquisition. Through this intensive and highly challenging Japanese learning process, I faced, struggled through, and overcame many difficulties, but this struggle actually led me to discover an inner strength and growing self-confidence that I had never previously tapped into or even known had existed.

Interestingly, I have observed the same phenomenon in my own Japanese students. Even though the class I teach is not an intensively paced one like the summer program at OSU, I try to present the students with a challenging curriculum structured much like the one I went through at OSU. Each semester it is very rewarding to see my (mostly) young students rise to the challenge and grow before my eyes, both in terms of their Japanese ability and their self-confidence as language learners. Without fail at the end of each semester's class I have students come up to me and thank me for the experience of the class. Although I do very much appreciate their sentiment, I know from my own experience that it is really the challenge and the process of language learning itself that is so empowering, not anything that I have done specially other than facilitate an environment that provides opportunity for my students to learn Japanese and hopefully grow as individuals as well.

As I was reflecting on these things on the last day of the summer session while also worrying about how I was going to pay for my upcoming fall tuition, as I had used up most of my saved funds during the summer quarter, Noda-sensei approached me with some very good, and quite unexpected, news.

"Jones-san, each year we award a scholarship to a student who demonstrates exceptional commitment and performance, and this year we are awarding that scholarship to you."

I was speechless and overcome with gratitude. The fact that I now had a means to pay my tuition for the upcoming year and continue my studies was reward enough. But to know that Noda-sensei, by far the strictest and most demanding teacher in the program, had recognized my effort was even more rewarding.

I was barely able to utter a proper "*Domo arigatou gozaimashita*" ("Thank you very much"). She just smiled and said "*Ganbatte kudasai*" (which is often translated as the Japanese equivalent of the English phrase "good luck" but which more literally simply means: "do your best").

Second & Third Year Japanese

Although the first-year summer Japanese intensive program had ended, I learned that the language department also offered an accelerated program that covered both second year and third year Japanese during a single regular school year. This meant two Japanese classes per day, five days per week, in addition to my other coursework.

Having gone through the summer intensive program with four hours of class per day, the pace of learning during the regular school year was a cakewalk by comparison, although in no way do I mean to suggest that the classwork was easy. Whereas during the summer program the only classes I had to deal with were my Japanese classes, during the school year I now had to balance my Japanese studies with my other classes, not to mention a part-time job to pay for rent and cover my daily living expenses.

Moreover, even while the pace of learning had slowed down a bit, the material itself only become increasingly more complex. I continued to struggle through 2nd and 3rd year Japanese, never quite feeling like I had a perfect grasp of the material, but I at least managed to keep pace with the course and get straight A's in my Japanese classes through sheer effort, and certainly not as a result of any natural talent for language learning.

One important thing that did change is that at some point, I truly began to enjoy the process of learning. In fact, outside of my earlier ceramics pursuits, Japanese was the first course of study that I had ever encountered that I truly enjoyed immersing myself in. Each new chapter in our textbook would introduce new grammar, new vocabulary, and new kanji, all of which would become part of my growing tool chest of Japanese. I believe another reason that I enjoyed my Japanese studies so much more than my other classes is that the study of Japanese, at least as the program was structured at Ohio State, was less about the "study" of the language and more about the "practice" of the language.

Indeed, perhaps what attracted me most to this course of study was that instead of simply reading endless textbook chapters and listening to boring lectures *about* the subject, I was actually *practicing* and *doing* the language, which I personally found to be much more stimulating and engaging.

Study versus Practice

This is an important distinction that new Japanese learners should be aware of. True learning of a language, Japanese being no exception, involves active *practice* more so than passive study. In this respect, foreign language learning more closely resembles the study of a musical instrument or practice of a sport than it does a college lecture class. As such, successful Japanese language learning requires a different mindset going in. You simply cannot approach the study of Japanese as you would a lecture class. Successful Japanese learning requires that you practice daily; you cannot simply passively take notes and then cram for the final at the end of the term.

I should also add that not all institutional Japanese classes are structured the same. Not all college or high school Japanese classes are structured like the ACT classes at Ohio State. Not every Japanese class at every institution requires that you stand up and act out the language. In fact, many Japanese classes *are* structured similarly to a lecture class, and as such, achieving a good grade in such classes may not require that you *practice* in order to prepare for and ultimately do well in such a class, at least in terms of getting a good grade.

However, and this is important, if you want to actually succeed in developing the *skills* of a successful foreign language learner (speaking, listening, reading and writing), then regardless of the structure of your class, it *is* absolutely essential that you *practice* the language, rather than merely study about the language.

....

If you want to actually succeed in developing the actual skills of a successful foreign language learner, then regardless of the structure of your class, it is absolutely essential that you practice the language, rather than merely study it passively.

....

Japanese Textbook Talk

Let me take this opportunity to discuss the Japanese textbooks used at OSU specifically, and textbooks in general. The textbook used at OSU was Japanese: The Spoken Language (JSL), authored by Drs. Mari Noda (my own professor at OSU) and Eleanor Jorden.

To say that JSL is a controversial and polarizing textbook is an understatement. The mere mention of JSL at any gathering of Japanese students and linguists is sure to incite a mud-flinging debate about the merits and demerits of this text and its rival textbooks.

The heart of the controversy over the JSL series is the fact that all four books in the series, which cover the equivalent of fourth-year Japanese, are written entirely in romaji and are completely devoid of any trace of the Japanese written language. For those that do not know, romaji is basically a written representation of Japanese using the English alphabet in place of hiragana, katakana, and kanji—the scripts that are native to the Japanese language.

Critics of JSL point to what they believe are two major flaws with JSL: the fact that the entire series uses romaji without introducing the native scripts, and the fact that the actual romaji system used in the books is somewhat unconventional and hard to decipher. There are also those who will say that the actual Japanese presented in the JSL series is overly formal and outdated. Still others frown at what they believe to be overly verbose grammar and usage explanations.

Although it is not my intent here to be an apologist for the JSL approach, as a product of the JSL system I would like to offer my own perspective based on my experience with this textbook, as well as the other learning materials I have used to learn and teach with over the years.

To Romaji or Not to Romaji?

First, let's address the issue of romaji. When it comes to use of romaji as a learning aid, the battle lines tend to be firmly drawn. Opponents of romaji insist that it has no place in learning Japanese; that it is a crutch that actually hinders the ability to become familiar with the native Japanese scripts; and that its use clearly signals an inferior teaching and learning approach.

Let me first clarify a common misconception about the JSL approach to learning. While it is in fact true that JSL is in fact written entirely in romaji, it is not true that students using this textbook do not learn to read or write the native Japanese scripts. Nor is it true that JSL learners end up using romaji as a crutch.

There is a companion series to JSL called Japanese: The Written Language (JWL) that is intended to be used concurrently with JSL, which introduces not only hiragana, katakana, and kanji using grammar and vocabulary sequenced with the JSL progression, but it also introduces those elements of Japanese that are unique to the written language. In other words, JWL is not simply an isolated introduction to each of the three Japanese written scripts, but rather, a comprehensive primer on the fundamentals of reading and writing Japanese. This is important because there are many conventions of the Japanese written language that are quite different from those of the spoken language, and so such a focused study is essential to ultimately gaining the ability to read and write Japanese.

As for the use or romaji in the JSL series, romaji is utilized in JSL along with notations that indicate the pitch accent of each word, so it can actually be a useful tool to help students pronounce Japanese more accurately. With respect to the unconventional romaji system used in JSL, which has been known to send students already used to other systems into fits of rage, there is a method behind this madness as well.

In contrast to the much more common Hepburn system of romaji, which attempts to most closely approximate the phonetic sound of the Japanese, the JSL system of Romanization, in contrast, attempts to follow the Japanese syllable structure rather than focus on the sound.

For example, the Japanese "ち" is represented by Hepburn Romanization as "chi", but in JSL as "ti". The former more closely approximates the actual phonetic pronunciation of the utterance, while the latter confines this and similar utterances to a two-roman-character representation.

The reality is that it is that the system of romaji used in any curriculum ultimately should not that big of a concern. It is a simple matter of familiarizing oneself with either system of Romanization, and debating the merits of the various systems ultimately ends up consuming far more energy than simply learning and adapting to whichever system is being used for a particular text or curriculum.

And while it is true that a student could theoretically attempt to learn and memorize Japanese exclusively using romaji to the detriment of learning to actually read Japanese, in practice this is not the case. The JSL series was created with the underlying pedagogical philosophy and approach to teaching that I have described in this book. When used in the context of this teaching approach, the emphasis is on active practice using audio and in-class performance (during which the textbooks are actually not allowed to be used), and so the true function of the JSL textbooks is really that of a reference manual. In this respect, the JSL series (particularly if used without using the accompanying audios) may *not* be the ideal textbook for self-study.

As to whether *any* system of romaji should be used at all, I'm personally kind of on the fence. Since I myself learned through the romaji-inclusive JSL system, I know firsthand that this approach to learning can be a highly effective one. Since the primary (although by no means exclusive) focus of the Japanese learning program at OSU (and similar programs that use JSL) is on the spoken language, whatever hindrance to learning to read the presence of romaji might have caused was (or should not have been) not that big of concern.

As Noda-sensei explained it to me when I expressed to her my own concerns that we weren't learning to read fast enough, the program at OSU was structured to mirror the language-development sequence of a young child. Noda-sensei pointed out to me that before young children learn to read and write they normally have about four to five years of purely spoken language development under their belt. Further, the written words and grammatical patterns a young child first learns are ones that the child should already be very familiar with. Although a formal academic foreign language learning program does not have the luxury of time to instill years of spoken language competence into its learners before even beginning to introduce the written language, the OSU program at least attempted to keep this "spoken-language-precedes-written-language" sequence intact.

While I do agree with this premise and have found it to be accurate in my own experience, I also believe there is something to be said for having learners gain familiarity, and thus comfort, with the Japanese written language as soon as possible. The textbook used at the college where I teach, the Genki Japanese series, is structured with this premise in mind. Romaji is used only in the first chapter. Chapter two introduces hiragana, chapter three introduces katakana, and then kanji is gradually introduced in subsequent chapters. From chapter two on, romaji is only used in the grammatical and usage explanations, not in the actual exercises.

The benefit of this approach is that it forces the learner to quickly familiarize oneself with the Japanese written language out of necessity and thus avoid the potential crutch of romaji. It also forces the student to develop his or her listening skills rather than rely on romaji to learn how words are pronounced. And it could certainly be argued that if the goal of a spoken-language-centered curriculum is to immerse the student in spoken Japanese as much as possible, why not also do so for the written language?

The potential drawback of introducing the Japanese written language immediately into the curriculum is the same as the argument not to do so: that doing so does not reflect the natural process of native language acquisition, in which spoken language acquisition far precedes written. Another drawback that I have observed is that requiring students to master the written language early on in the process while they are still struggling mightily with the basic spoken elements can result in information overload that some students simply cannot cope with, which can and does lead in some cases to otherwise motivated and capable students giving up in frustration.

My own personal verdict based on my years of experience as a learner in a romaji-inclusive environment and as a teacher in a romaji-exclusive environment is that I favor an approach somewhere in the middle of the two extremes: giving priority to first mastering the spoken components of the Japanese language with a more gradual introduction of the written components, leaving romaji behind only once students have had a reasonable amount of time to assimilate and gain a level of comfort processing the language using written Japanese only.

Too Keigo or Too Casual?

Another topic of discussion when it comes to the merits of Japanese textbooks is the underlying levels of formality of the language introduced in them. Some textbooks take a more "casual" approach to the language, catering to the mindsets of the mostly young students who comprise the student demographic, while others place a strong emphasis on mastery of the various levels of formality that are unique to the Japanese language.

One of the criticisms of JSL is that the language introduced in the series is overly formal and outdated. While it is certainly true that language evolves over time and the JSL series could benefit from a revision that more accurately reflects today's language, I disagree with those who criticize the excessive focus on the more formal styles of Japanese speech. In fact, for reasons I will discuss later on in this book, I would argue that the JSL series' detailed emphasis on the various levels of formality in general and formal speech in particular is one of the book's strengths.

You see, when it comes to formalities and honorifics in Japanese, even new Japanese company recruits fresh out of college often require a crash course in polite speech (called "*keigo*" in Japanese). Foreign learners of Japanese who fail to receive training in this unavoidable component of the Japanese language are often unable to properly assimilate and use *keigo* once their formal Japanese education has ended. Although once my own formal education ended and I was living in Japan the majority of my interactions with friends and other Japanese I encountered occurred using the more casual forms of speech (which, by the way, are also fully covered in JSL), when in business or other formal situations requiring the use of honorific speech, my exhaustive training in the OSU program using the JSL series served me very well in Japan and continues to serve me well in the present day in my daily life and business career.

Whether or not you ultimately require the use of highly formal speech will depend upon the Japanese social context you find yourself operating within. While you may find yourself primarily in social settings that do not require extensive use of *keigo*, you certainly do not want to find yourself in a situation where Japanese social convention requires that it be used but you are unable to due to neglect to study or lack of exposure to this vital aspect of Japanese speech. Therefore, concentrated study and practice of the various levels of formality and the contexts in which they are used, a strength of the JSL series, should be an essential component to any well-designed curriculum.

Characteristics of a Good Japanese Learning Program

The bottom line is that there is no magic Japanese textbook or other learning material on the market that is significantly better than all of the others. Any textbook, software, website, app or combination thereof that contextually introduces Japanese usage and grammar, speech patterns, vocabulary, and the elements of the written language in a logical progression can be effective tools for learning.

More important than the textbook is the pedagogical approach and learning environment used to teach the lessons contained therein. For example, at the college where I teach, the language department determined the textbook that we used to teach with (Genki Japanese) and the chapters to be covered at each level, but otherwise left *how* the material was taught to each individual instructor.

When I was initially hired at the college where I teach but prior to teaching my first class, I sat in on the class of several of the instructors to get a feel for how the material was being taught at the school. I was surprised that unlike the program at OSU, which was highly structured, other than using the same textbook there was no common approach to how each teacher taught the material. While I taught the material based on the training I had received at OSU, some of the teachers taught the material in a somewhat of an "open-book" style that I personally considered to be more appropriate to teaching a group of kindergartners than a class of college students.

My point here is that the textbook used is far less important than the pedagogical approach and curriculum design of the program. The JSL textbook series can be highly effective when taught using the underlying pedagogical approach behind which it was created. But if used devoid of that approach and taught in a less-structured manner, it is doubtful that the learners would gain the same benefit. Likewise, any other decent textbook can be an effective one provided the methodology behind teaching it is sound.

Thus, here are just some of the elements you should look for when searching for an effective formal learning program:

- Grammar and elements of speech introduced contextually in a logical progression

- Heavy reliance on use of audio media in the learning process

- Emphasis on practice and performance of language in and out of class (using audio media and in-class drills)

- Incorporation of written language that (at least initially) follows the content and structure of the class's spoken component

- Study of the conventions of Japanese that are unique to the written language

- Practical introduction of vocabulary focused around scenarios a student is likely to commonly encounter in real-life situations

- Thorough coverage of the various levels of formality in the Japanese language

- Study of unique Japanese social conventions embedded in the language

- Immediate corrective feedback from instructor when errors are made

- Emphasis on active participation and *practice* and actual use of the language

- A well-defined pedagogical approach consistently followed by all instructors

Although you may not have the luxury of shopping around for the ideal Japanese learning environment, to the extent that you do, let the above guidelines serve as a starting point to help you find a learning curriculum best suited to your personal needs and goals.

Now, getting back to our story, by the time I had completed third-year Japanese, an interesting phenomenon had begun to occur. While I continued to struggle with the new material in my current classes, I noticed that the material I had struggled with in first and second year Japanese would continue to pop up and be recycled into the new material.

I later learned that this was due to: 1) the intent of the curriculum designers and textbook authors, who understood that earlier material needed to be constantly recycled and reviewed; and 2) the nature of language itself, in that the basic foundation of grammar and vocabulary learned early on in the process is in fact real Japanese that continues to be used even as Japanese grammar and usage becomes increasingly more complex.

What was most interesting is that the material I struggled mightily with and was hopelessly unable to fully grasp in first-year Japanese at some point "clicked," to where it registered somewhere in my brain and I finally "got it," to where you could say that I now had mastered that grammar or vocabulary.

In fact, I now know that this too is part of the language learning process. You struggle with new material and most likely, you will never quite "master" it while you're initially learning it. Then you will go on to more advanced material and struggle with that as well. However, the older material you struggled with earlier will appear repeatedly as part of your new material, and at some point that older material will "click" and you will find that you now have a thorough grasp of it. This pattern of initial struggle and delayed mastery will repeat throughout your language learning process, both inside the classroom and out in the world once you are in a Japanese-speaking environment.

Thus, having managed to struggle through 2nd and 3rd year Japanese, I could see that I had made quite a bit of progress in less than a full calendar year, even while being painfully aware of how much further I still had to go.

Fourth-year Japanese

Toward the end of the school year, I received some exciting news. For the first time, fourth-year Japanese would now be offered at OSU as part of the summer intensive program. That meant that I had the opportunity to complete all four years of Japanese offered by my college within a single calendar year. This was a pretty big deal to me considering that I had expected I would need an entire additional school year to complete my Japanese studies, even though I had close to enough transfer credits to have graduated otherwise. Needless to say, I signed up immediately, and couldn't wait for the summer intensive session to begin.

Whereas in Japanese 102 the previous summer there were about 25 students in my class, by fourth-year Japanese attrition had set in and there was only about 12 of us remaining. I remember fourth-year Japanese as being significantly more difficult than the first three years, and as the summer wore on, a number of my classmates began dropping out one by one, to the point where by the end of the summer there were only about seven of us left.

One great thing that happened during the summer session was that I made my first real Japanese friend, Nana-san. Nana-san was a physical education professor from Saga University in Japan's Saga Prefecture, who was attending Ohio State on a research fellowship.

I met Nana-san in the language lab. She overheard me working diligently with my oral tape practice, and introduced herself to me. She offered to help me with Japanese in exchange for helping her with English. I eagerly accepted her offer, and was able to learn a lot from Nana-san even outside of the class. I discovered how invaluable it can be to have a native Japanese friend/tutor/language exchange partner to provide help and feedback in a much more unstructured and relaxed environment away from the classroom.

Nana-san also introduced me to her friend Sayoko-san, also from Japan, whose husband was working on a PhD in fine art at OSU. I invited Sayoko-san and Nana-san to dinner at my house, and furthered my friendship with both of them. I made a clumsy attempt at making Japanese food for them, which they politely ate but I'm now sure that inwardly they probably did not enjoy that much.

This episode reminds me of an interesting phenomenon that has occurred many times during my stays in Japan, where I've often been invited to dinner by families of friends I have met. On these occasions, I always looked forward to enjoying some authentic Japanese home-style cooking, only to find myself treated to such American delights as Thanksgiving-style turkey dinner, spaghetti and meatballs, and even homemade pizza.

Somehow in their attempt to be as hospitable as possible to their foreign guest, my warm Japanese hosts decided the best way to accomplish this would be to attempt a meal from my native country, not realizing that what I really had hoped to experience was authentic Japanese cuisine.

It was during these occasions that I regretfully wished that I had treated Nana-san and Sayoko-san to my own tasty homemade pizza instead of my lame attempt at sushi and tempura!

A couple weeks into the summer intensive program, Noda-sensei made an announcement to our class. There would be an opportunity to study abroad in Japan for a year at Tsukuba University beginning the upcoming fall quarter.

I had known I wanted to travel to Japan in some capacity but I was so immersed in my study that I hadn't given serious thought on how I was actually going to accomplish this. Suddenly, here was a real opportunity. Furthermore, Japan's Ministry of Education would be providing visiting students with full-tuition scholarships plus a monthly stipend and even round-trip airfare.

Needless to say, this was the ideal situation but there was just one hitch. Once fourth-year Japanese was complete I would be done with my undergraduate studies and therefore no longer eligible to take part in this foreign exchange program. However, I discovered a loophole: provided I simply did not apply for graduation, I was still technically an undergraduate, and therefore eligible for the program.

With this knowledge in hand, I went ahead and applied for the exchange program, and soon after learned that I, along with seven other classmates, would be leaving for Japan that September for a study year abroad!

PART 2:
Study Abroad in Japan

I remember how nervous and excited I was with anticipation at my coming year in Japan. I had never traveled outside of the U.S., and I had no idea what to expect. Predictably, I made some serious newbie traveler errors. In addition to packing two full suitcases, I shipped two enormous boxes full of clothes, cooking utensils, and even toiletry items. All of this was overkill, as Japan is a completely modernized society where naturally every item of necessity is readily available for purchase.

In contrast to me was a friend of mine from OSU, Mike, who was also studying in Japan but at a different university, International Christian University (ICU) in Tokyo. Mike was an ex-marine who had already lived in Japan for several years during and following his military stint, and was therefore a seasoned traveler. I remember visiting Mike at his Tokyo apartment and being flabbergasted by how few items he had brought with him: a week's supply of socks and underwear, a few shirts, a couple pairs of pants, a single coat, and a suit, all of which easily fit into a single, modest-sized suitcase.

Taking a tip from Mike, in subsequent trips to Japan I have grown progressively better at reducing my baggage volume, but I still tend to over-pack so here's a tip for first-time travelers to Japan: bring with you only the bare essentials. You can buy pretty much whatever items you need once you get to Japan.

Anyway, back to our story. Our OSU foreign exchange group hopped a quick commuter flight from Columbus to Chicago, and then we had to wait for a couple of hours before we finally boarded the enormous 767 bound for Japan.

My previous longest flight had been a five-hour domestic coast-to-coast flight. The flight from Chicago to Japan, in contrast, would be over 14 hours. After chatting excitedly among one another about what was to come once we arrived in Japan, we settled into the eternal duration of the flight. After watching all of the available movies and reading my books and attempting unsuccessfully to sleep, there were still several hours left on the flight. By the time our plane was on approach to land at Narita International Airport outside of Tokyo, we were an entirely exhausted group of travelers.

First Impressions of Japan

My first view of Japan was from the window seat of the plane as it approached the airport for landing. The landscape was dotted with small houses with unusual roofs not found in the U.S. We flew over rice paddies tended by farmers wearing broad-rimmed basket hats and driving pickup trucks so small they looked like little toys across unimaginably narrow little strips of road that cut perfect squares through the rice paddies.

Once the plane landed, we disembarked in a sleep-deprived haze and made our way through immigration. From the moment I stepped foot in the airport I could tell I was in an entirely different culture.

Impeccably dressed female airport attendants guided the passengers down the concourse in the most exceedingly polite fashion I had ever experienced. After lining up at immigration, I presented my passport at the immigration window, affirmed that I was there to study for a year, and was allowed to pass through as a legal visitor to Japan.

After collecting our baggage and passing through customs inspection, we made our way to a bus that would take us to Tsukuba.

By now we were all thoroughly exhausted, and as excited as I was to take in the surrounding landscape, I'm sure I was not the only one who collapsed into a deep sleep for the entire bus ride to our destination.

Japanese Foreign Exchange

By the time we arrived at Tsukuba, it was already evening. We got off the bus with our luggage, and wondered where to go next. Actually, prior to our trip we had learned that each of us would be assigned a Japanese "tutor," who would not only help us with our Japanese, but help us get settled into our new environment.

Our tutors were waiting for us as we got off the bus. We introduced ourselves to them using the formal, polite Japanese we had diligently practiced during our course of study at OSU, and were baffled when the group of tutors began laughing hysterically at us.

We soon learned that the level of speaking formality used among Japanese college students is not necessarily the same as that practiced in our classroom. It was only the first of many revelations to come. Having completed four years' worth of Japanese, by the time I left for Japan I felt like I had a pretty solid grasp of the language. I was therefore shocked to discover that I could barely understand anything our tutors were saying to us or each other.

It turned out that my "universe" of known Japanese grammar and vocabulary was limited to only that which I had studied in college, and even though that was quite a bit of Japanese, I was now in the middle of a massively larger universe of Japanese that I did *not* know, which was now overloading my senses to the point where it all blended together like meaningless white noise. My brain went into panic mode as I realized that I didn't know nearly as much Japanese as I thought I did.

As far as our tutors went, it was pretty hit or miss. Some of the exchange students were matched up with attentive, enthusiastic tutors who became close friends and in some cases, even romantic partners. My own tutor found me and introduced himself to me as Daisuke. Daisuke was a nice enough guy, but he turned out to be a pretty indifferent tutor. We had very little in common and in fact, throughout the year I ultimately ever met him only a handful of times. He did take me to get some furniture and household items on my first full day in Japan, so I appreciated that at least, but as far as helping me learn Japanese, Daisuke was not all that helpful.

Once we arrived on campus, we were led to Ichinoya, the dormitory that would be our home for the next nine months. Japan and Japanese people are nothing if not accommodating to their guests, and as foreign visitors, we were given the privilege of living in the best dormitory on campus.

Our rooms were relatively spacious, had a single Western-style bed, and included a private toilet and shower. The dorms in which most of the Japanese students lived, in contrast, were much older, much smaller, and had neither a shower nor a toilet, or even a bed. Japanese students living in these dorms slept on futons, shared a communal bathroom in their building, and bathed in the communal campus public bath.

I suppose the faculty in charge of assigning our rooms thought that we foreigners might have difficulty adapting to Japanese customs like sleeping on the floor with a futon and bathing in the communal bath. I remember feeling a bit spoiled by my relatively luxurious living quarters, but I was grateful all the same for the familiar creature comforts.

Life at a Japanese University

Having settled into my dorm room and begun to acclimate myself to campus life, I looked forward to the start of school. Officially we were all assigned to the International Relations Department. Tsukuba University is a unique college in that it is welcoming to *"kikokusei,"* or returning Japanese students who spent several years abroad and were fluent in English. Therefore, in addition to the classes taught in Japanese, the International Relations Department also offered classes for these students taught entirely in English.

Eager to accelerate my Japanese learning, I opted instead to enroll in courses taught in Japanese, but soon found that I could understand almost none of my professors' lectures, and overwhelmed, I quickly ended up dropping these courses. Actually, since as I mentioned earlier I had already completed my graduation credits, I didn't technically need to take any classes. Of course the University expected me to enroll in the requisite number of classes. However, an interesting aspect of Japanese universities is that for Japanese students it is incredibly competitive to gain acceptance to a top university (of which Tsukuba was one), and in order to do so, in addition to their compulsory education most Japanese youth spend years attending cram schools called "*juku*" in order to prepare for the rigorous entrance exams that determine the fate of aspiring college students.

However, once students actually gain acceptance to a university, all but the most studious begin what essentially amounts to a four-year vacation. Having studied non-stop for their entire youth in order to get into a college and facing the prospect of a life of endless and tedious working hours as a salaried employee upon graduation, since the top Japanese companies make recruiting decisions based more on their college than what they studied while they were there, many Japanese college students use their time in college to enjoy what will likely be their only extended break from constant work and study that they will ever have an opportunity to take until they retire.

The result of this system is that many Japanese college students blow off their studies entirely, and instead concentrate on developing their social lives through "circles," which are basically school clubs centered on various hobbies and pursuits. For instance, at Tsukuba, there were tennis circles, music circles, tea ceremony circles, martial arts circles, calligraphy circles, and circles for just about every other imaginable type of activity.

Most Japanese students pick a circle in their freshman year, and then this circle becomes the center of their social lives as well as their college activity for the next four years. In fact, at the beginning of each school year, each college has a school festival, called a "*gakuensai*," during which circles actively (and quite aggressively I might add!) recruit new incoming freshman to join their circles and thus, became a part of that social clique.

Since this was the Japanese way and since I had no real obligation to attend classes, I admit that I adopted this approach to Japanese college life, and essentially ended up blowing off my lecture classes apart from the Japanese language classes. I was still very motivated to improve my Japanese, and so I couldn't wait for the Japanese language classes to begin. However, from the very first day of class I experienced a rude awakening.

Although Tsukuba University is well-regarded as a top institution for the quality of its Japanese language instruction, I found my Japanese class to be very below the level of my classes at Ohio State in terms of quality and effectiveness, at least from my perspective. For one thing, our main grammar class had over 100 students, so it was essentially a giant lecture class. Perhaps we would be called on once per class, if even that, and the rest of the time there was nothing to do but just watch passively as the other students took their turn answering a question posed by the instructor. I felt like I wasn't learning anything or even doing anything, and frankly, was just wasting my time in this class.

Other classes were smaller in size and somewhat more useful, but compared to the intensive, well-structured, performance-based instruction I received at Ohio State, this was extremely deflating, and despite the fact that I was as motivated as ever to improve my Japanese, I realized that improvement was not going to come, at least for me, from the classroom environment at Tsukuba. After a few short weeks, I even stopped going to my Japanese classes, and decided to find a way to improve my Japanese on my own.

Successful Japanese Self-study

Having resolved to go at it alone, I knew that my first task was to tackle kanji. One of the interesting things about my foreign exchange experience was that there were many exchange students from schools all over the U.S., not to mention students from South Korea, China, the Philippines, Africa, the Middle East, and many other parts of the world.

Naturally, I was curious to see how the Japanese ability of our OSU group stacked up with the Japanese of students from the other schools. One of the other groups of students was from Stanford. After mingling with these students for a while, it was clear that the Stanford students were far advanced in terms of their reading ability. Stanford's upper-level students were apparently already reading novels in Japanese, something that was far beyond the ability of even those of us who had already completed 4th year Japanese at OSU.

However, in terms of speaking ability, it was clear that the OSU students were the crème of the crop in terms of speaking ability compared to students of the other American colleges. No one illustrated this difference more than Theo, a student from Stanford.

Theo had an impeccable reading ability, and was already translating professionally on the side. He could flawlessly read any text you put in front of him, and we were all enormously impressed by his ability. The most impressive demonstration of Theo's ability came one night when we gathered in his room to watch a video of the movie Chungking Express by Wong Kar-wai.

The thing about this video was that it was in Chinese with Japanese subtitles, and most of us could not understand Chinese or read Japanese fast or proficiently enough to have any hope of understanding the movie. No problem though. Theo interpreted the entire movie for us without ever missing a beat. It was a very impressive performance indeed (Theo that is, not the movie, which I found to be just OK).

Despite Theo's performance when reading Japanese, when you took away the written text, he was barely able to put a coherent sentence together. Several of the other Stanford students were in a similar boat. They could read at a very advanced level, but most of them were relatively deficient when it came to conversing on the fly, and quite a few had surprisingly awful pronunciation to boot.

The OSU group was pretty much the mirror opposite of the Stanford group. Those of us who had made it through fourth-year Japanese were relatively fluent from a conversational standpoint and our pronunciation was quite on point, but we couldn't read a block of Japanese text to save our lives.

This contrast of abilities does not reflect any differences in the innate capability or intelligence of the students, but rather, the difference in emphasis in the respective curriculums, and this is an important point for all prospective Japanese language learners to consider:

Research your institution's curriculum, so that you know what the focus of your learning will be. The reality is that when it comes to Japanese, four school years (or in my case the equivalent of four years of classes crammed into one calendar year) are simply not enough to fully cover all aspects of the Japanese language. Therefore, the instructors who design the Japanese curriculums at each school are forced to make choices: some institutions, such as Stanford, at least at that time, opt to focus more on the written aspect of the language at the expense of the spoken aspect, while other institutions, such as OSU, choose to focus on the spoken language, but at the expense of development of kanji acquisition and reading ability relative to some other schools.

These choices of emphasis on the part of the language programs represent, consciously or unconsciously, the pedagogical philosophy of each language department. In the case of OSU's language department, the philosophy was a clear and conscious choice: spoken ability should precede reading and writing ability, since this approach mirrors the natural progression of a young child learning his or her native language.

As I mentioned earlier and as Noda-sensei elaborated when we used to argue for more kanji instruction, a young child will normally have, from birth until about the age of four or so, almost exclusively focused on speaking ability, and so children are actually quite fluent in the language, in fact far much more fluent and advanced than a fourth-year language student, before they even begin formally learning their ABCs.

The OSU program was designed to mirror this natural learning progression. While I couldn't argue with Noda-sensei's logic, I was not alone among the OSU students in feeling quite deficient in terms of our reading ability, particularly once we saw how we stacked up with the Stanford students.

It was against this backdrop of perspective that I realized that one of my main tasks for my year at Tsukuba would have to be seriously improving my reading ability in general, and kanji knowledge in particular.

Conquering Kanji

Motivated and determined to learn to read, I decided to give myself an assignment that I thought would be an ideal way to develop my reading skills: I would read through an entire Japanese novel, and when I encountered a word or kanji I didn't know, I would simply look it up and write it down in my notebook. I figured that by the time I worked my way through the entire novel, I'd have a pretty good grasp of the written language.

The novel I chose was *Hard Boiled Wonderland and the End of the World* (世界の終りとハードボイルド・ワンダーランド), by Haruki Murakami. I choose this novel since I had read it several times in English, and had also picked up a copy of the original Japanese version at a Japanese bookstore. I figured I was so familiar with the material that this would help me get through the unfamiliar Japanese.

Well, even though this seemed like a good plan in theory, it ended up being a complete failure in practice. After about four hours of intensive study with my novel in the library, I had managed to work my way through all of one-half of the first page!

I quickly realized that this method of learning was not going to work. The main problem was that every time I came upon a kanji or kanji compound (a combination of two or more kanji) that I was unfamiliar with, which was basically every third character or so, I would have to put down the novel and go look up the character.

As you may know if you have any experience studying kanji, kanji are essentially pictograms, or symbols that may contain or suggest meaning, but which do not appear to offer clues as to their reading. This is in contrast to hiragana and katakana, which are the Japanese language's two phonetic alphabets (commonly referred to as syllabaries), which represent the phonetic sounds of the Japanese but in general offer no inherent universal meaning at the single-character level.

The difficulty in looking up unfamiliar kanji is that unlike looking up an unfamiliar word in the dictionary, where you can at least identify its spelling and reading and go right to the dictionary definition with ease, with an unknown kanji you cannot look it up by its reading since you have no idea what the reading is.

Instead, in order to look up a kanji for which you do not know its reading, you have to look it up based on its radical. A kanji radical is a sub-element of the kanji character used to group with other kanji with the same radical.

Therefore, when looking up a kanji based on its radical, you must first identify the radical itself. Sometimes this is not clear, as the kanji may contain more than one element that could potentially be used as the radical. For example, in the following image, the grey areas indicate the radicals for each kanji.

Once you have identified the radical, you must then count the number of strokes in the radical, and then additionally, count the number of strokes used to write the character overall, and then go to the index in the dictionary, search for the radical based on its number of strokes, and then once you find the radical, sift through all of the characters grouped by that radical until you find the group with the same number of strokes as the character you are looking up, and then finally, sift through *that* group of characters until you find your character, at which time you can finally find out what the reading of the character is.

Sound confusing? Sound complicated? Sound time consuming? Indeed it is! After only getting through a mere half-page after four hours of concentrated effort, I was exhausted and frustrated. I realized then that the fundamental difficulty in learning to read

Japanese was that kanji are by nature opaque in terms of identifying their readings. In other words, when looking at a kanji, it may offer some clue as to its meaning if you are familiar with or can identify the meaning associated with the character. However, there is apparently nothing in the characters, at least to the untrained eye, that offers any clue about how to read them.

Therefore, when attempting to read through a text, without a clue as to the reading, each time you come upon an unfamiliar kanji character, this kanji acts like a barrier or wall that halts your reading progress until you go through the laborious process described above of looking up the character, and there was no way around this process. If I were to at least know the reading of the kanji, even if I didn't understand the meaning of the compound (word) or even the character itself, then I could at least simply look it up relatively quickly and painlessly based on its reading. However, with no clue as to the reading, there was no away around the time-consuming process of looking up the character by radical.

Frustrated and realizing that I didn't have the willpower to stick to my original plan, I abandoned my attempt at reading through a novel as a way to learn to read Japanese, and was at a loss for how to proceed.

Tokyo, Akihabara, and the Word Tank

One thing that initially helped the kanji lookup process was the purchase of a Canon Word Tank electronic dictionary. I bought this dictionary in Akihabara during my first trip to Tokyo with my fellow students. It might be enlightening if I provided you with a synopsis of this entire trip, which represents my impressions as a first-timer in Tokyo.

Since there was no direct train connecting Tsukuba to Tokyo at that time (now there is, the Tsukuba Express, which runs from Tsukuba to Ueno Station in Tokyo), we boarded a highway bus for the hour-plus ride to Tokyo.

Up to this point my only experience in Japan had been Narita Airport and Tsukuba City in Ibaraki Prefecture, which was quite remote. I was completely unprepared for the enormity and density of humanity and overall sensory overload of Tokyo.

Our first destination was Sensoji Temple in Asakusa, Tokyo. Sensoji Temple is Tokyo's oldest temple and most visited by Japanese and tourists alike. Sensoji is perhaps most famous for the *Kaminarimon* entrance gate with its enormous red lantern.

Once you pass through this gate, you enter Nakamise, an outdoor strip of shops selling every imaginable type of Japanese-themed gift and trinket, including folding paper fans, toys, traditional Japanese sweets, kimono, and even authentic Japanese swords!

Although looking back most of these trinkets were mere souvenirs targeting foreign tourists, I remember taking the bait and buying an assortment of colorful paper fans, silk handkerchiefs with ukiyo-e motifs, little paper lanterns, and key chains. Years later, I still have many of these items, and they actually have made nice little mementos of that time.

Making your way past Nakamise, you come to the temple grounds. There is a well where visitors rinse their hands for purification prior to entering the temple. There are also little stalls where visitors can receive an *"omikuji"* paper fortune for a "donation" of 100 yen.

Finally, you climb a massive staircase leading to the temple itself, where most visitors make a small monetary offering before saying a prayer. I took all of this in with fascination. Although I'd been in Japan for about a month, for the first time I felt I was *really* experiencing Japan.

After visiting the temple I, along with a group of students, enjoyed a tasty meal of tempura udon noodle soup. After lunch, we had the rest of the day to roam about Tokyo freely. However, the thought of exploring Tokyo on my own was completely intimidating, as I had no clue how to navigate Tokyo's complex network of trains and subways.

Fortunately, our friend Theo had been to Tokyo before, and so we followed his lead. He led us to Akihabara, which was originally famous as Tokyo's electronics district, but today is perhaps better known as a center of otaku culture full of shops selling anime, manga, video games, action figures, and even maid cafes.

Theo wanted to visit one of the giant electronics stores and purchase an electronic dictionary. Up to that point I didn't know a thing about electronic dictionaries, but I ended up purchasing the one he recommended, the Canon Word Tank.

This versatile dictionary had built-in Japanese-English and English-Japanese dictionaries, as well as a *"kokugo"* Japanese dictionary with Japanese definitions. All of these functions were incredibly useful, but by far the most important function of this dictionary for me was the *kanwa* (kanji lookup) dictionary.

Using the *kanwa* dictionary, it was possible to look up a character by entering its reading, if you knew it, or if not, by its radical and/or non-radical parts. For example, entering "KAN" in the reading field would bring up all characters that shared that reading. From there, you simply scrolled through until you found the character you were searching for, in order to find out all remaining info about that character.

In this example, the reading "KAN" is shared by about 160 characters, or 20 screens worth.

If in addition to "KAN" you entered 3 in the radical field to indicate a kanji with a reading of "KAN" and a radical of 3 strokes, this would reduce the number of screens to 7. If you further could identify the total number of strokes (including the radical strokes), this would likely bring you to the exact character you were looking for, or at least reduce the candidate characters to a single screen or two.

On the other hand, if you did not know the reading (the main difficulty of kanji discussed earlier) but could identify the number of radical strokes and number of total strokes, you could enter that information and narrow your search in that manner.

For example, let's say you wanted to search for the reading of the character 実, which has a 3-stroke radical and 8 strokes total. I would enter 3 in the Radical field and 8 in the Total Strokes field, while leaving the Reading field blank.

Doing this first brings up 3 screens worth of possible 3-stroke radicals. The radical portion, the little "roof" that caps the rest of the character, is found on the first screen and is designated as "B". So, by pressing "B" on my keyboard, this brings up two screens worth of all characters containing that specific 3-stroke radical and corresponding 8-stroke characters.

From there, it is a relatively simple matter to find the character. Once found, selecting the character and pressing the "Jump" button on the keyboard would call up a screen providing all of the essential information about that character, including its meanings, all of its possible readings, usage examples, and even more importantly, all compounds (character combinations) with that character as the lead character.

Thus, by looking up the 実 character, it was easy to discover that the *onyomi* (traditional Chinese) reading is *JITSU*, while the *kunyomi* (Japanese) reading is "*Mi*" as well as "*Mino*" when used as a verb with a hiragana る on the end.

In case you weren't aware, one of the difficulties of mastering Japanese kanji is that most kanji contain at least one *onyomi* and one *kunyomi* reading, and many kanji contain several of each type of reading. The only real way to know which reading is the correct reading is through learning the various uses of the characters.

As a general rule, when multiple kanji are combined to form compounds, in the overwhelming majority of cases the readings of each character will be one of the *onyomi* readings (although you still have to learn precisely *which onyomi* reading is being used for a particular compound when there are more than one.

There are, however, plenty of exceptions to this rule, where the combined characters take on the *kunyomi* reading instead. For example, the character combination 足跡, which means "footprint," is read "*Ashi-Ato*," both which are the *kunyomi* readings of their respective characters.

On the other hand, when a character is read in stand-alone fashion, or when it is combined with hiragana characters, usually to form verbs and adjectives, usually the reading will be a *kunyomi* reading, although again even with this knowledge in hand, in many cases one still needs to confirm precisely which of several possible *kunyomi* readings is the appropriate one for that particular combination.

In contrast, although the Chinese language requires more total characters to be learned in order to read the language at a reasonable level, each Chinese character only represents a single reading, and so in some respects one could argue that it is easier to learn to read Chinese than it is to learn to read Japanese.

This combination of there being multiple readings of single characters combined with the fact that there is no apparent information cluing the learner as to what the reading might be is what makes learning kanji so difficult, and why it is commonly agreed that Japanese is the world's hardest written language to learn.

The Word Tank made the lookup process much easier and more versatile, and quickly replaced my enormous 1600+-page Japanese Kanji Character Dictionary that I had purchased in the U.S. prior to my trip and lugged all the way to Japan.

The Word Tank was much lighter and compact, fitting easily in my pants pocket, and so I carried it around with me everywhere

I went. Now, whenever I came across a character I was unfamiliar with (which in the beginning occurred a couple dozen times a day at least), I could simply whip out my Word Tank and look it up.

Likewise, if I was talking to someone in Japanese and I didn't understand a word they were saying, I could now simply enter it into the Word Tank and get up to speed right then and there.

Of course today we live in a world of computers and smartphones, with tons of websites and software programs and perhaps most importantly, apps that make the Japanese learning process much more accessible and instantaneous. However, back in 1995, the Internet was in its infancy and cell phones, much less smart phones, had barely begun to reach the masses. From the perspective of a 1995 Japanese language learner, the Word Tank was a gift from the heavens. And in fact, I still have my trusty old Word Tank, and still occasionally use it to look up a word or character even to this day!

So the Word Tank was the first major breakthrough in enabling me to begin to learn to read and recognize kanji at a much faster pace, and I highly recommend that you take advantage of similar electronic dictionaries, software, and smart phone apps to support and accelerate your own learning process.

Now a little bit more about my first visit to Tokyo. After purchasing my Word Tank, Theo led us to Shibuya. When we first got off the bus in Tokyo at Asakusa I was overwhelmed by the sheer number of people all around us, but even this could not begin to prepare me for my first Shibuya experience.

We got off the Yamanote Line at Shibuya station and instantly found ourselves on the train platform enveloped by a massive surge of people. It was all I could do to follow our little group out of the station through the station Hachiko exit out into the plaza facing Hachiko Crossing, famous as being the world's busiest human intersection.

All around me were people, people, and more people. Towering over me were walls of neon and huge video screens blasting ads for an assortment of cosmetics, energy drinks, and recording artists. The sensory overload was unlike anything I had ever experienced, or could have possibly imagined.

Once the Walk signal lit up and we began crossing the intersection, I was nearly in a blind panic as a tsunami of hundreds of people quickly descended upon us from all directions. I felt for sure I was going to be trampled in a stampede, and was shocked and relieved that we made it unscathed on the other side of the street.

Even today, having since crossed Hachiko Crossing dozens of times, I still have no idea how so many people converging into the intersection from so many directions manage to weave among one another without serious bodily carnage. Hachiko Crossing is certainly on my list of man-made world wonders, and something every visitor to Tokyo absolutely must experience.

Having made it to the other side of the intersection, the suffocating crowd of people by no means abated as we made our way through Center Gai, a narrow maze of alleys filled with hip boutique shops and restaurants. At one point I got separated from our group and again panicked, thinking I might never make it back to our returning bus later that night. However, I managed to spot one of my classmates up ahead and made sure to stay glued to my group from that point forward.

Today, I navigate around Tokyo on my own like second nature. But from the perspective of a guy who grew up in the considerably more sparsely populated Midwest, there was no way to prepare myself for the enormity of Tokyo and its sheer volume and density of people. Today I love the city and still get excited whenever I visit, but at the time of my very first visit, I was in pure panic and survival mode.

A System for Memorizing Kanji

My purchase of the Word Tank represented a breakthrough in my ability to look up and learn kanji more efficiently, but it still wasn't enough. The second breakthrough came when I visited my friend Mike from OSU about whom I wrote earlier, who was attending International Christian University in Tokyo.

During my second trip to Tokyo, I paid a visit to Mike. Since Mike was my *sempai*, already having lived in Japan for several years, I mentioned to him my kanji learning woes.

Mike smiled and showed me the system that he had developed and used to memorize kanji himself. What he showed me was a single bound notebook. Inside the notebook, he had divided each page into columns of 10.

At the top of each column, he wrote a character, and underneath that character, its essential meanings, and underneath that, its readings. Then, underneath all of this information, he carefully wrote out each character 10 times.

Mike explained to me that when he was learning kanji, each day he studied 10 new characters, while reviewing the previous 20. He said that he spent the better part of a year using this system to learn all 1,945 Joyo Kanji, the set of kanji characterized as being required for daily use in Japan.

Mike said that he dedicated a good two or three hours each day of study using this method, and it enabled him to reliably gain the ability to recognize, read and write the characters. He further explained, in the authoritative tone of the ex-Marine that he was, that there were no shortcuts to learning kanji: you simply need to put in the work.

For me, Mike's system was just what I needed. I was willing to put in the work. What I was lacking was an organized, logical system for learning kanji. Mike's method seemed to fit the bill perfectly. Having attempted to learn kanji by reading my way through a book, I encountered the issue unique to kanji that I touched on earlier: because of the opaque nature of kanji, there is no way to discern the reading of unfamiliar kanji, and the time consuming and exhausting look-up process made studying in this way wholly impractical.

I realized that it would be more efficient in the long run to put in the time to thoroughly memorize the characters before I attempted to read them in a body of text. That way, at least I would have an educated clue as to the reading of unfamiliar kanji compounds when I came across them, and with the ability to actually read the character combinations, even if I wasn't sure what they meant I could at least now look them up quickly as I would an unfamiliar English word.

Excited, on my way home to Tsukuba I purchased my own notebook, and could hardly wait to begin my own full-fledged kanji study the next day.

Studying Kanji

At Ohio State, Noda-sensei, the head of the Japanese language department, was a very strong proponent of learning the language in context, and indeed, that was how the curriculum at OSU was structured. The textbooks that Noda-sensei co-authored, Japanese: The Spoken Language series were all designed so that students would learn new grammar, usage and vocabulary in the context of authentic dialogues and sentence patterns.

Therefore, we focused on developing our Japanese skills through the practice of full dialogues and drills consisting of sentence structures, which we practiced inside and outside the classroom in a contextual manner.

This philosophy extended to the department's approach to teaching the written language, as reflected in the companion textbook to the Spoken Language series: Japanese: The Written Language.

Using this textbook, the written language was introduced in the form of written passages of text that reflected words and phrases that we had already learned through our spoken-language study. Kanji too was inserted into these passages, and always consisted of kanji representing words we already knew. Within the Japanese curriculum at OSU, there was never any thought of attempting to memorize all Joyo kanji characters in rote fashion devoid of context, or beyond the scope of Japanese that we had already learned.

Looking back on my time at Ohio State, I can clearly see the logic of this approach. The reality is that four years of Japanese college instruction at best provide a foundation for more advanced learning later on: there is simply no way to cover all the Japanese one will eventually need to know.

From this perspective, I believe that the approach used at Ohio State was a good approach. However, at the time I was impatient to learn more kanji, and by the time I arrived at Tsukuba, I was painfully aware of the limitations of my kanji and reading ability. As I described earlier, I had attempted to apply the principles of learning kanji in context on my own by reading my way through a novel, and in fact, a novel that I was very familiar with in English, and found this to be excessively difficult and wholly inefficient.

I therefore came to the realization that at some point in the Japanese learning process, it is unavoidable to have to bear down and memorize the essential kanji. The learning in context approach worked fine as long the learning progress was confined to a known, contained universe consisting only of everything we had learned so far through our coursework.

However, out in the real world beyond the classroom walls lay a universe that contained all the Japanese I did know, which was quite a bit of Japanese, but which also contained an infinitely vaster universe of all of the Japanese which I did not know.

This was particularly true when it came to kanji. The reality I was faced with was that there were many more kanji (and kanji compounds) that I did not know than there were kanji I did know. Furthermore, although many Japanese language learners tend to become overly preoccupied with learning kanji, as they certainly have a right to be, the reality is that simply learning kanji does not mean that you will thereafter have the ability to actually read Japanese.

This is because learning kanji is somewhat akin to learning ABCs. If you only were able to recognize, say, 8 of the 26 letters of the alphabet, you would have a very difficult time filling in the blanks and reading actual words, unless you were a wiz at Wheel of Fortune. You might be able to recognize all of the words written using only the 8 letters you were familiar with. But every time you encountered one of the remaining 16 letters you were not familiar with, you would have no hope of being able to read that word.

Such is kanji. Now, the comparison is not perfect, in that while in the case of the alphabet, the letters themselves generally contain no meaning and must be combined to form words, many kanji, by themselves, are words. Kanji, unlike the letters of the alphabet, also contain suggestions of meaning, provided you are familiar with the associated meanings, and so this can at least give you a clue as to what a kanji or combination of kanji might *mean* even if you are unable to read them.

However, more often than not, kanji are combined with other kanji to form nouns, or else they are combined with hiragana to form verbs, adjectives, or even compound verbs (normally a combination of two kanji plus the hiragana する or できる), such as 勉強する (*benkyou-suru*: to study).

Therefore, just as not knowing 16 letters of the alphabet would clearly throw a wrench in your ability to even begin to read words and discover their meanings, not knowing the readings and associated meanings of, say, 1000 characters also will ultimately inhibit your ability to read Japanese at any level approaching literacy.

Knowing the individual kanji enables you to recognize the readings of kanji when they are used in combined form, so that you may *then* learn the actual meaning of those compound words that are formed using kanji. But in order to do so, it is first necessary to learn the kanji themselves just as it is necessary to learn the letters of the alphabet in order to form and read words.

Now, with this said, the task of learning all existing kanji is all but impossible. Therefore, Japan's Ministry of Education has assigned a list of characters, called the Joyo kanji (originally 1,945 but currently 2,136), which all Japanese students are required to learn.

The vastness of this undertaking is reflected in the time required by native Japanese speakers to learn these kanji. While speakers of English learn all 26 letters of the alphabet in kindergarten, Japanese students continue learning the Joyo kanji all the way through secondary school.

In this respect, the "learn kanji in context" approach taught at OSU appears to reflect to the way Japanese learners themselves learn kanji. That is, by the time a Japanese student learns a kanji at a given grade level, chances are good that he or she is already familiar with at least some of the words associated with that character, and so already has a background of context for its use.

The foreign language learner, in contrast, does not have the luxury of nine+ years of time to learn all of the Joyo kanji in such a manner, and thus, will at some point require a more intensive and accelerated process in order to cover the Joyo kanji at minimum in order to handle the majority of written Japanese he or she is likely to encounter out in the real world.

The Kanji Crossroad

With a realization of the necessity of the task at hand, I made the choice to bear down and do the work. Now is a good time to point out that the study of kanji very often represents a crossroad in the learning journey of Japanese language students. Essentially, Japanese language learners can be broken down into two groups:

1. Those who learn their kanji and become literate

2. Those who do not learn their kanji and remain functionally illiterate

There are countless gaijin out in the world today who are highly fluent in spoken Japanese but who are functionally illiterate when it comes to reading. However, there are comparatively few who are functionally literate as a result of having thoroughly mastered kanji.

Of course there are also those like my classmate Theo (at least at that time) who were functionally literate while not necessarily being fluent. In fact, this is actually not uncommon among Chinese learners of Japanese, who bring a complete repertoire of kanji to the table and generally are able to use their kanji background to grasp the written language at a much quicker pace than the spoken language. However, among Western learners, this is a relatively rare occurrence.

Thus, at some point in your language learning career, you will find yourself at this crossroad, and will have to decide whether or not you will commit to learning kanji so that you can become literate in Japanese, or whether you will be content with being fluent but functionally illiterate or at best having very limited literacy.

The reality is that most Japanese learners ultimately buckle at the overwhelming task of "learning their kanji" and end up remaining functionally illiterate readers even if they become fluent speakers. Most such learners know at least some kanji, and so are not completely illiterate. Very few, however, commit to the kanji learning process to the extent that they gain functional literacy.

Now, I should perhaps mention what Noda-sensei once pointed out to me, which is that in reality, even most advanced foreign language learners that do succeed in studying their way through the Joyo kanji are not truly able to read *everything*.

Indeed, as I discussed earlier, learning kanji means that you have a grasp of the pieces of the puzzle, but not necessarily that you have solved the entire puzzle. What normally happens, rather, is that a kanji-capable Japanese learner will ultimately gravitate toward one or more specific fields of knowledge, and develop functional literacy in those areas, but not necessarily in written Japanese outside of those fields.

For instance, in my own case, I have a solid grasp of at least the Joyo kanji and am comfortable reading IT manuals, business contracts, financial reports, newspaper articles, and most novels, but I become pretty lost whenever I have to read anything, say, medical-related. This is because I simply do not possess a functional vocabulary of medical-related words since I have little to no exposure in this area.

Other learners who master the Joyo kanji may gravitate toward biology, environmental studies, technology, business, finance, or any other area or group of areas. Some may simply use their kanji capabilities so that they can enjoy reading manga or novels in a fluent manner.

The point is that even most highly advanced learners of Japanese will likely become functionally literate in some areas, while not so much in other areas, so in this respect, it certainly *is* possible to not have mastered all of the Joyo kanji while still becoming functionally literate in a narrow area of interest.

With this overview of the kanji learning process in mind, let me now return to my own experience studying the Joyo kanji using the method I learned from my friend Mike.

The Ultimate Kanji Study Method

Here, in a nutshell, is the kanji study method I used to successfully learn the Joyo kanji in a relatively short period of time. First, you'll need a source for all of the Joyo kanji. Nowadays you can easily find a listing of the Joyo kanji on the Internet, through a kanji learning app, or a traditional kanji textbook. This listing should provide you with all of the kanji info, including each character's meaning(s), reading(s), and stroke order (how to write it using the proper sequence of strokes, which is important in order for the kanji to come out looking right when you write it).

Next, you'll need a standard notebook. On the first page of the notebook, use a ruler to divide the page into 10 columns. Then draw a vertical line across the columns to create a line at the top, so that you'll write the character to be practiced at the top. Underneath the top entry, draw another field in which you'll write the meaning of the kanji, and under that field, draw one more field large enough to contain the possible readings. Then, in the remaining space below, draw vertical lines across leaving enough space to create fields in which you can practice writing each character 10 times.

For your first day of kanji study (make sure to date each page so you have a record of your progress), write out each of the first 10 kanji you will study.

For example, depending upon the source book you use, the first 10 characters you study on your first day may be as follows:

日 一 人 年 二 大 本 三 中 四

Your list may be entirely different from the above, but what is important is to simply make sure you cover all of the characters in some progressive, logical order. Since the order of presentation in most books begins with the simplest and most commonly used characters, it is usually logical to simply follow this order.

Next, underneath each character entry, you would write the character's basic meaning or meanings. Thus, under 日 you might write: Sun, Day.

Underneath this entry you would write the character's *onyomi* and *kunyomi* readings. For our example, we would write something like:

Onyomi: NICHI, JITSU

Kunyomi: hi, -bi, -ka.

(Depending on your personal preference, you can write these using katakana for *onyomi* and hiragana for *kunyomi*, as is common in textbooks, or if you are not allergic to romaji simply write them using romaji, as is done above.)

Finally, underneath these entries you would begin to practice writing out the actual character, following the prescribed stroke order. Practice carefully, writing each character out 10 times.

As an added step that was not originally included in my friend's method, I also recommend writing out into your column at least one compound that you are familiar with that contains the kanji you are studying. If you aren't familiar with any compounds containing the kanji, then use a dictionary to find one that appears like it will be a useful word to know, ideally containing an additional character that you have already studied. This added step will add context to your process and also help you build up a vocabulary of compounds using the kanji you studied.

Repeat this process until you have covered all 10 characters to be studied for the day. Now, having written out each kanji, spend time studying each character one by one. First read through your entries and retrace the characters. Next, close your eyes and visualize the character, its meanings, its readings, and how it is written.

Next, repeat this review and visualization process for each of the 10 characters. You should plan on spending at least an hour or two of study each day. You can also certainly keep your notebook with you and review sporadically throughout the day as time allows, but you will need to at least plan on spending an hour or two of highly concentrated and undistracted study.

Repeat this process on the second day with your next set of 10 characters, but also allot perhaps 10-15 minutes or so to *review* the previous 10 characters from the prior day. You'll likely find that you have pretty good recall based on your previous study, but that you'll find some aspects of some characters that you have forgotten. No problem, as that's simply part of the process.

On the third day, study your next set of 10 characters as you have done on the first two days with your first two sets, but now also allot about a 20-minute review for your previous day's 10 characters and also the 10 characters from two days ago.

As you review, again follow the initial process of reading over each kanji entry, and then close your eyes and go through the visualization process of recalling the information for each character.

Once you have cycled a set of 10 characters through your initial study, your concentrated next-day review, and your quick third-day review, you should by now have a pretty solid grasp of that set of characters. Keep in mind that unless you have a photographic memory you will never be able to recall every single bit of information of every kanji. However, this process should at the very least provide you with a solid basis of knowledge of the characters you have covered.

After performing the three-day study cycle for each set of 10 characters, you can essentially leave that set alone as you move on to subsequent character sets, but you should also occasionally do a quick review *all* of your previously learned characters. This review can consist of simply glossing quickly over your older character entries in order to refresh your memory.

Since there are 2,136 Joyo kanji, if you study 10 characters per day, every day, you will have covered all of the Joyo kanji in 214 days. I realize that may seem like a long time, but on the other hand, it is less than a year's worth of effort, and considerably less time than the nine years or so that Japanese students devote to learning the same number of characters.

If you make the commitment and follow this system, you will find at the end that you will now have a solid foundation of kanji knowledge that will enable you to quickly attain literacy in the Japanese language.

As a result of the effort made in persisting through with this approach to kanji acquisition, you will be able to identify the meanings and readings of most kanji you encounter in written Japanese. Even if you are not entirely sure of a reading (such as in a case when there are multiple possible readings), you will at least be able to make an educated guess as to a kanji or kanji compound's possible reading. You will also be able to gain a sense of what a compound might mean even if you are unsure of its reading, based on the work you have done in familiarizing yourself with each character's suggested meaning.

There is an additional benefit of having done this practice that most Japanese instructors and linguists do not teach or perhaps are not even aware of. We have already discussed the fact that kanji are by nature opaque, and do not appear to offer clues as to their readings.

However, over the course of your concentrated kanji study, you will eventually begin to recognize repeating patterns of shapes, with corresponding readings that are either the same or similar to one another.

For example, in the following character set:

招　召　昭　沼

All contain the common element 召 (which is itself a kanji character), and all have an *onyomi* reading of "SHOU".

As a result of your concentrated kanji study, you will begin to recognize similar patterns along with their common readings, which will help you to recall the readings when you encounter these types of characters in written text.

Although these patterns do not apply to all characters, there are enough of them that offer clues as to the kanji's reading as to make the reading process much easier as a result.

Is the above method the best method for learning kanji? I cannot say. At the time it was presented to me it was by far the most promising approach that I had found. Today there are plenty of Internet kanji learning resources as well as software and smartphone apps, all of which can help facilitate the kanji learning process.

What I do know, however, is that when it comes to learning kanji, no book, Internet site, software, or app can take the place of hardcore study, and that at some point every Japanese learner ultimately must buckle down, put in the work through sweat equity, and commit to learning kanji.

When it comes to learning kanji, no book, Internet site, software, or app can take the place of hardcore study, and at some point every Japanese learner ultimately must buckle down, put in the work through sweat equity, and commit to learning kanji.

I can say that although there are many fine online resources for kanji study, I highly recommend that as part of your study/memorization process you actually write out the characters by hand, even if you do not plan on handwriting kanji in your daily life. Indeed, even many native Japanese speakers rely on word-processing software and smartphones to write kanji, and I often hear Japanese friends remark about how they have forgotten how to write many kanji by hand simply because they never have occasion to do so anymore.

My own kanji handwriting ability has likewise suffered. Although as a result of my initial kanji study I did learn to handwrite kanji, over the past decade or so I'd estimate that 99% of my Japanese writing has been done on a computer, and as a result my handwriting ability has slowly deteriorated over the years. Nonetheless, although I'm no psychologist I believe that writing out the kanji as part of the study process creates deeper neural-patterns that will enable you to remember and recall kanji better than if you simply study passively by looking at a screen without writing the characters out.

A reasonable question to ask at this point may be: is it worth that much effort to learn kanji? That is indeed the million-dollar question. The answer all depends upon what you want out of your Japanese study. If you simply want to be able to converse with friends and perhaps watch anime and films or listen to J-Pop in the original Japanese, then maybe you do not need to become literate in Japanese. If that is the case, you can forgo the extended effort required to learn kanji.

If, however, you desire to be able to read Japanese novels, newspapers, manga, and to be able to be functionally literate so that you can live or work in some professional capacity in Japan or for a Japanese company without being hampered by your inability to read, then you may find the one-time investment in your time and energy to pay off handsomely.

In my case, what was the effort I spent studying my kanji worth? Well, learning to read kanji has given me the ability to work as a professional translator, doing what I love in the form of writing and immersing myself in Japanese each day, working from the comfort of my own home at the hours of my choosing. In sheer monetary terms, learning kanji has enabled me to earn a very comfortable full-time income over the past 15 years or so. Learning kanji has also given me the opportunity to teach Japanese to others, which is another thing I love doing. It has enabled me to work as a consultant, helping Western companies sort through Japanese paperwork and vice versa, and as a researcher finding and presenting information in Japanese about many fascinating subjects. Having learned my kanji has also given me the ability to enjoy reading novels and manga and Japanese magazines and newspapers and websites, not to mention the ability to communicate via email and social media with Japanese friends, acquaintances and business associates.

An additional and important benefit of learning kanji not to be overlooked is the ability to develop an advanced spoken vocabulary. Much of spoken-language vocabulary acquisition comes from the ability to read. Even in one's native language, there tends to be a vast difference in the spoken vocabulary of one who is highly literate, and one who is illiterate or only barely literate. The same is naturally true of Japanese. By having the ability to read Japanese, you will likely develop a much broader and more advanced vocabulary than one who is merely able to speak the language but who is not able to read it.

Finally, bear in mind that it is not necessarily an all-or-nothing issue of whether or not you choose to learn kanji. Most college Japanese programs cover at least a reasonable portion of the Joyo kanji, and knowing even one-fourth or one-half of these kanji is certainly better than not knowing any at all. And if the program I outlined earlier seems too intense or you aren't able to make such a concentrated investment of time, you can always go at your own pace. For instance, instead of studying sets of 10 kanji characters per day, you can study sets of five, or three, or even one.

The important thing is to find a pace you can sustain and most of all, BE CONSISTENT and PERSISTANT IN YOUR STUDY. Stay the course, even at a snail's pace, and eventually you *will* gain mastery of kanji.

All of these are factors you should consider when you reach the crossroad in your own Japanese learning career and must decide whether or not learning kanji is worth your while.

Getting back to my own story, I used the above method and stuck to it diligently throughout the year. I put in two hours of concentrated study at the library each day learning my new characters and reviewing my previous characters. Then in the evening I would spend an hour per day back at my dorm room reviewing.

It was grueling but satisfying work. The more I studied, the more I was able to read, and at the conclusion of the process, which actually lasted until I was back home in the U.S. the following year, I knew that I had done the work that only a fraction of all Japanese learners would ever be willing to do. Looking back, it is hard to believe I was able to summon the energy to put forth that kind of effort, but at the time I felt it was simply what I had to do in order to continue progressing in Japanese. Today, words can't even describe how grateful and happy I am that I did.

PART 3

Mastering Spoken Japanese beyond the Classroom

Mastering Japanese Social Relationships

Back at Tsukuba, I had resolved my kanji-learning issue, but an even bigger issue loomed: I had to find a way to advance my Japanese speaking ability. As much Japanese as I had learned in my brief time at Ohio State, once I landed on Japanese soil I was painfully aware at how woefully inadequate my spoken Japanese still was. And having discovered that the structured language classes at Tsukuba were not going to be of much help, I knew that there was only one way to truly improve my Japanese: make Japanese friends and find a way to communicate in Japanese on a daily basis.

Since I was at a college campus, one might assume that this would be an easy matter. However, I found that making Japanese friends required overcoming some unique aspects of Japanese culture and social structure that made this task more difficult than I could have imagined.

Making Japanese Friends

During my first full day in Japan, as I was walking across the campus, I was surprised and even a bit dismayed that every single Japanese student seemed to be blatantly ignoring me. Now, it is not as though I expected them all to come up to me, shake my hand, give me a hug, introduce themselves to me and wish me a pleasant stay.

However, it was clear that as I walked past my Japanese counterparts, they were studiously avoiding making eye contact with me, as if to ensure that they would not have to interact with me on any level. As I looked around though, I began to realize that it wasn't just me they were avoiding eye contact with. They were also avoiding eye contact with one another.

It took me a while to realize that this avoidance of eye contact with unfamiliar people is simply a normal aspect of Japanese culture and society. Unlike in the West, where it is customary to make eye contact with and even nod and say hello to complete strangers as a gesture of friendliness or even common politeness, in Japan, Japanese habitually make a concerted effort to *not* make eye contact with strangers, as doing so in Japanese society conversely can be considered to be invasive or even rude.

Nowhere is this cultural tendency more apparent than on a crowded Tokyo commuter train. Even in rush hour, with bodies sandwiched against one another, two Japanese who are strangers to one another may be physically inches apart but psychologically a universe away from one another.

In Japan, you'll rarely see Japanese strike up casual conversations with people they don't know while waiting in lines at the grocery store or the bank, or while seated on a commuter train, as we often do in the West.

I do not know the precise origins of this social orientation. It could very well be that because Japan, particularly in the cities, is so densely populated, the habitual avoidance of eye contact evolved simply as a way to maintain a semblance of privacy where there otherwise was none. The important thing for you to realize is that this custom exists, and know going in that you will likely have to negotiate it as well as several other uniquely Japanese social conventions in order to form relationships with Japanese people in Japan.

Negotiating Japanese Social Conventions

The careful avoidance of eye contact in Japan could in part also be a byproduct of the *"uchi-soto"* social orientation that exists in Japanese culture. Japan is often called a "group-oriented" culture. Where as in many western cultures the development of a unique individual identity is considered a desirable trait, in Japan, conversely, it is not individuality, but rather, participation in, belonging to, and conformity toward specific social groups that is considered desirable. In the simplest terms, *"uchi"* (内 inside) refers to being within a group, while *"soto"* (外 outside) indicates being outside the group.

All Japanese belong to various social groups. These groups may be a group of friends, a family, a school class, a college activity circle, or a company, just to name a few. As a general rule, Japanese people will tend to be more open and relaxed toward those within their group (内) and more closed off and distant to those outside of their group (外).

The *uchi-soto* distinction is also reflected in the Japanese language itself. If you are already in the process of learning Japanese you may already know that one of the unique characteristics of the Japanese language is its multiple, distinct levels of politeness and formality. That is, the form of language used in any situation is dictated by its social context.

Another determining factor in the style of language Japanese speakers use in speech is the *"joge-kankei"* (superior/subordinate) social relationship. Whereas *uchi-soto* indicates one's position (inside or outside) relative to a given group, *joge-kankei* reflects hierarchical levels of superiority and inferiority, or relative social status even within the same group. In both cases, the relative social relationship of the involved speakers (and persons being referenced in a dialog) determines the form of speech used in the conversation.

For example, when using the verb that means "to be" to describe oneself or another person being here (or there, or somewhere...), the choice and form of verb that is used depends upon the relationship of the person being described to the other people being referenced in the context of the situation.

In Japanese, the dictionary definition of "to be" is the verb "*iru*," and this casual form of the word is typically used among friends of the same age, among family members, and by a person of a superior position speaking (and referring) to an inferior, just to name a few examples. A somewhat more neutral and distal version of this verb, "*imasu*," would commonly be used among two people who do not know one another well and who are unsure of their relative social positions. A much more formal word with the same meaning, *irasshaimasu*," would be used by a person of an inferior position to address or refer to a person of a higher status (such as a subordinate to his boss or a sales clerk to a customer). Finally, there is yet another, humble-polite word with the same meaning, "*orimasu*," which a person of perceived inferior status would use to refer to oneself in relation to a person of a higher status (same examples as "*irasshaimasu*" but with the person now speaking in reference to oneself).

Another example of varying levels of formality that reflect the relative formalities of social relationships in Japanese speech is the use of honorific titles. Even most people with no extensive knowledge of Japanese are familiar with the honorific title "-san" (such as Tanaka-san or Suzuki-san). Yet there are additional levels of honorifics affixed to Japanese names, and how these are used is again governed by the relative social relationship of the individuals being addressed or referred to. In addition to "-san," which is a relatively neutral honorific, there are others. "-Sama" is used in place of "-san" to address or refer to persons of elevated status in much the same way that "*irasshaimasu*" is used in place of "iru" or "imasu" in the above example. For example, members of Japan's royal family, are, by default, referred to using "-sama" rather than "-san". Similarly, "-chan" is used as a diminutive, affectionate form of address toward or in reference to (usually) females with whom one has a close relationship with. "-Kun" is similarly used in reference to men, and also by superiors in a company addressing or referring to subordinates.

The above are just a few examples and by no means an exhaustive study of how the relative status of social relationships is reflected in the Japanese language, but the *uchi-soto* and *jogei-kankei* social conventions are two of the primary factors that govern the various levels of formality used in Japanese speech.

Generally, members within a group (内) will tend to interact with one another using a more relaxed, casual manner of speech (but *joge-kankei* and other factors will ultimately determine what style of speech is actually used). In contrast, by almost universal custom Japanese will opt for a more formal, polite, and distant form of speech when speaking to someone outside of their group. Likewise, persons of elevated social status will tend to interact with inferiors using a more casual form of speech, and vice versa.

For example, a company president will normally address his own employees using a very informal style of speech, but in making a sales call to a client, this same high-ranking individual would adopt a highly honorific form of speech when speaking to a customer, reflecting the fact that in the first case, he is communicating with members within his group, and in the second case, he is communicating with members outside of his group.

Likewise, a company department manager will normally address her subordinates using a casual form of speech, but then turn around and address (or refer to) the company president using a highly formal style of speech, thus reflecting her relative social status in each respective hierarchical relationship (*joge-kankei*) even within the same group (the company).

Such Japanese social conventions are extremely complicated subjects for which an exhaustive study is beyond the scope of this book. What is important to realize here, beyond puzzling together how to negotiate them properly when actually communicating in Japanese, is that these unique aspects of Japanese culture often makes it difficult for foreigners to immediately form relationships with native Japanese, and vice versa. Many foreign visitors who lack a basic understanding of these social conventions find the apparent distantness of their Japanese counterpart off-putting, and many uninitiated visitors mistakenly conclude that Japanese are cold and unfriendly.

In fact, this is not actually the case. Rather, the primary difficulty of forming relationships with Japanese in Japan is not that Japanese dislike foreigners (although like in any culture there may certainly be some who do), but rather that the initial default relationship between foreigner and native Japanese is an *uchi-soto* relationship whereby the foreigner starts out from a position of being on the outside of the most basic Japanese social group: being Japanese.

The challenge in forming relationships with Japanese people, therefore, is finding acceptance into a social group. Once entrance has been gained inside a group (again, depending upon the nature of the group this group could contain hundreds of people, such as a company, or involve just a single other person), a foreigner can in most cases expect to find their Japanese counterpart to be warm, kind, friendly, and open.

In my own case, even though I had studied about this *uchi-soto* group orientation in college, this was the first time I had encountered it in a real-life situation, and even with my background knowledge, I had to conquer the irrational sense of somehow feeling shunned by the very people I was hoping to interact with.

Added to the challenge of discovering that by default I was on the outside looking in was the fact that I was by nature a shy introvert. One of the side benefits for me of learning Japanese was that it forced me to take the initiative in speaking up, and this experience of "speaking up" in class was, for me, quite empowering in that it had boosted my confidence and improved my ability in taking the lead in initiating communicating with others. In fact, even today as a result of my years of Japanese study I have two distinct personalities: my quiet, introverted English-speaking personality, and my relatively outgoing Japanese-speaking personality.

However, in unfamiliar situations I still tended to quickly revert to my shy, introverted self. Now, at Tsukuba and facing a situation where I found myself on the "outside" of what seemed to be the entire Japanese population, the prospect of overcoming this social barrier felt all but impossible, and I remember being deflated by the realization that it was going to be very difficult for me to form Japanese social relationships in Japan.

Cracking Japanese Social "Circles"

One way I attempted to make Japanese friends and form relationships was by joining a circle. Since I played tennis recreationally back at OSU, at the invite of a girl I met at a school dance I joined one of Tsukuba's several tennis circles, thinking that I would naturally be able to make friends through tennis.

I was in for a harsh surprise. What I did not know was that among the several tennis circles at Tsukuba, my circle, called "Forrest," was the most hardcore and almost militant in its approach to the game.

The circle met for "*asa-ren*" (early-morning practice) from 6 to 8 two mornings a week, even during the winter months. Throughout the entire practice, members would repeatedly scream "*faito*" (fight!) almost as a battle cry. Forrest members were entirely devoted to the pursuit of tennis excellence. However, they did not appear to be the least bit interested in international relations. To this day I do not know why they allowed me to join their circle, but although I became a member of Forrest, I still found myself as a complete outsider, and just as I described earlier almost all of the members avoided making eye contact with me or having anything to do at all with me.

I later learned that there were other tennis circles (and circles for other activities) that were far-more laid-back and welcoming toward their foreign members. However, I hated to be a quitter and ended up sticking with Forrest, despite the fact that with a couple of exceptions, I never ended up making friends or barely even interacting at all with the other members.

Indeed, my experience with Forrest illustrates that in Japanese society it is possible to be inside the group on the surface, while still being very much outside the group in reality. One example of this is a company employee who comes to be regarded by the organization as useless. Due to Japan's custom of lifetime employment, such employees are not fired. Instead, they are given a desk by a window, which symbolizes that all they are expected to do from that point forward is enjoy the nice views. Or in some cases, shunned employees may be put in charge of a department with no work to do and no subordinate employees. These workers are, on the surface, still a member of their group (the company), but for practical purposes, they are very much on the outside of the group.

I would later encounter similar experiences to my Forrest experience in different social settings, and eventually learned to not take it personally. I simply learned to accept the fact that in such instances, I was, from the perspective of my counterparts, outside of their group, and as such, had no reason to expect them to be outgoing and friendly toward me.

There are a couple lessons to take away from my experiences. The first is to understand the basic nature of the *"uchi-soto"* distinction of Japanese society. Although you may find yourself "on the outside looking in" in many Japanese social settings, it is important to not take this personally and wrongly conclude that Japanese people are unkind.

The second piece of advice is that if you want to make friends with Japanese people, chances are high that in most instances, all initiation of friendship and relationship forming will have to come from you. While there are certainly exceptions, such as young Japanese who have lived abroad or have had prior exposure to foreigners, Japanese people in general are simply not wired to be friendly and outgoing toward people they do not know, and when it comes to interacting with foreigners, many Japanese do not know how to handle this situation and so simply opt to avoid dealing with it altogether.

Finally, despite my Forrest story above, the best way I've found to get on the "inside" and form true relationships with Japanese is to find a way to become part of a group, whether this be a college circle, a company, a class, or any other social environment in which you can become an involved member.

If you can absorb the above advice, you will have a very good chance of forming many meaningful and long-lasting relationships with Japanese, because the other side of the coin is that once you finally *do* manage to gain acceptance on the inside of a social group, you will often find that your Japanese counterpart has become a devoted friend for life.

The happy news for me is that despite my initial unsuccessful attempts at being accepted into a group, I ultimately succeeded in making friends, although it wasn't easy. In fact, during the first three months of my stay in Tsukuba, I was very discouraged by the fact that I still hadn't made one Japanese friend.

I instead found opportunity to communicate in Japanese with a group of exchange students from South Korea. Unencumbered by Japan's rigid social customs, the Korean students I met at Tsukuba were exceedingly friendly, and since most of them did not speak English but were relatively advanced at Japanese, Japanese became our common language of communication. We made a habit of studying together and hanging out quite a bit, and so this was the initial way in which I was able to practice Japanese in Japan.

Interesting, this phenomenon of exchange students banding together to practice their language of study with one another rather than with native speakers is not limited to just something that occurs in Japan.

Having lived in San Diego, California for the past several years, I have observed the same phenomenon on American soil. With its idyllic climate, San Diego is a prime destination for students of English from abroad. Time and time again, I have seen groups of exchange students from various countries practicing their English with one another rather than with native speakers of the language. I believe this illustrates the common difficulty most foreign visitors to a country who are still struggling with the language have in meshing with native locals.

I believe there are at least a couple clear reasons for this struggle. The first is the language barrier. Not having confidence in the local language, the foreign student finds the prospect of initiating conversation with locals intimidating. Another reason is that while foreign language students come to a new country in hopes of making friends with and communicating with locals, most locals tend to be preoccupied with their daily lives and simply do not share the same interest. The end result is that foreign exchange students in a country are often left with only one another as their means of improving their language and communication skills.

Such an outcome is not necessarily a bad one, at least in the beginning. However, there is an additional outcome that is significantly worse, and unfortunately, all too common in foreign language learning situations.

Avoiding the Gaijin Herd Mentality

While at Tsukuba, I was hell-bent and determined to find a way to communicate in Japanese, but many of my peers were apparently not quite as determined. Perhaps my fellow exchange students came to Japan, like me, with the initial intention of making Japanese friends and communicating in Japanese. However, when, like me, they encountered the same obstacles, most opted for the path of least resistance, and simply spent the rest of the school year hanging out with the other English speakers.

The result is that most of these students did not significantly improve their Japanese at the end of their year abroad. Many even became disillusioned and ended up washing their hands of Japan completely as a result of their initial experience in Japan that did not meet their high expectations.

I've witnessed the same thing time and time again in San Diego as well. I've seen Japanese exchange students here for four years of college who instead of making the effort to make friends with native English speakers, simply spent their entire four years banding with other Japanese-speaking students, and as a result, were barely able to speak English even after four full years abroad.

The lesson here is that if you truly want to improve your Japanese language ability during your time in Japan, you must avoid this path of least resistance, even when the going gets tough. Those who persevere and make a concerted effort to use and improve their language skills as well as to make friends with locals are the ones that ultimately succeed in becoming advanced users of the language.

The most extreme example of a successful and determined language learner that I have ever encountered (aside from myself perhaps!) was my friend Katsu, a Japanese male who was living in San Diego a few years ago. Like me in Japan, Katsu also initially encountered the same difficulties in making friends with locals and was at first frustrated at his lack of English improvement.

About midway through his four-year stay in the U.S., Katsu decided that he was not going to speak another word of Japanese while on English soil. From that point forward, not only did he succeed in making local friends, but he even insisted on speaking only English to his Japanese friends.

Although many of his Japanese friends complained to me that it was inconvenient and awkward to always be communicating with Katsu in English, which resulted in some cases in him becoming distanced from those friendships, in the end, by the time he returned to Japan Katsu had significantly improved his English, while most his Japanese friends went home not having improved at all.

I was not quite as militant in my approach as Katsu, but I did make it a point to avoid hanging out excessively with the other English speakers and instead focused on finding more opportunities to make Japanese friends and spend as much time as possible speaking Japanese.

My first real breakthrough in making friends with Japanese came around New Year. Three months had passed since arriving in Tsukuba, and by then I was quite frustrated and depressed. I still hadn't made any real friends. I felt that my Japanese wasn't improving at all. Christmas was approaching. I missed my family and had never felt lonelier in my life. On top of that, I became sick.

I was dreading the prospect of spending the holidays sick and alone at Tsukuba. Almost all of the Japanese students would be returning to their hometowns and many of the exchange students would also be flying home, so I was facing the prospect of an extremely lonely, isolating stretch of days in a college campus ghost town.

Fortunately, the International Relations department organized a homestay opportunity for the foreign exchange students who were remaining in Japan. Those interested would be introduced to a Japanese student who was willing to host us at his or her family's home. Grateful for the opportunity to have a chance to visit a real Japanese family and desperate to leave the Tsukuba campus during the holiday, I eagerly signed up.

I was introduced to Ryushi, who would be my homestay host. Ryushi was a sophomore who was majoring in education. Ryushi lived in Kyushu, so I would be visiting his hometown of Nagasaki.

Ryushi was really nice and friendly as well as patient with my still-limited Japanese, and I was grateful for the opportunity to visit his family.

Since he was planning to leave campus at the conclusion of the school term, I was to take a train by myself and meet up with him again in Nagasaki about a week later, a couple of days before New Year's Eve. As I mentioned, during this time I became very ill. Hanako, a *kikokusei* (a returning student from abroad) who had been friendly to us exchange students and who was still on campus, thankfully drove me to the hospital. I received medication but I still had a very bad case of the flu.

A quick amusing sidebar about this hospital visit that illustrates how limited my Japanese still was at this time. When the doctor came in he said to me: "*Nete kudasai.*" Panicked, I turned to Hanako and explained to her that I could not follow the doctor's instruction because I was not sleepy. She and the doctor both burst out laughing, and then she explained to me that while "*nete kudasai*" indeed meant "go to sleep," what the doctor was actually saying here was simply: "please lie down."

Even with my flu medicine, I spent Christmas alone in bed, physically sick and emotionally depressed. I had reached the bottom and for the first time considered giving up and going back home. I was honestly too sick to travel but I simply couldn't bear the prospect of spending the rest of the holiday season in Tsukuba, so even though I still had a terrible case of the flu and was too weak to even think about traveling, I decided to go to Kyushu anyway and just pray that I would get better in time.

Japanese Homestay

Unfortunately I was not feeling better by the time I boarded the bus to Tokyo, from where I took the Shinkansen bullet train to Kyushu. I slept almost the entire time and was barely able to appreciate the fast but ultra-smooth ride of the bullet train or keep my eyes open to take in the exquisite scenery as we passed by Mt. Fuji.

By the time I arrived in Nagasaki, I had a burning fever and could barely walk, but I was determined to hide my illness and make the most of my homestay opportunity.

Ryushi met me at the station in Nagasaki and we walked to his home. Since Kyushu is in southern Japan, it was thankfully quite a bit warmer than Tsukuba, which by the time I left there was blanketed in snow.

When we arrived at Ryushi's house he introduced me to his mother, as well as his teenage sister and three young cousins, who were also there visiting for the holidays. Ryushi's mom was very kind, but with the sister and the cousins it felt like de ja vu all over again as they couldn't deal with the unfamiliar presence of a foreigner and ultimately avoided me like the plague for my entire stay.

Later in the evening, Ryushi's father came home from work. The father was a typical Japanese salaryman. He worked as a reporter for the local newspaper. He smoked like a chimney and loved to get his drink on as well.

The father was also friendly and very inquisitive about me and my life in the U.S. We chatted for hours, or perhaps I should say we had what on the surface appeared to be a conversation but which was in reality pretty much a one-sided conversation consisting of the father talking and me unable to grasp 90% of what he was saying.

I nearly burned out my Word Tank looking up all the words I didn't know in a frantic attempt to keep the conversation going. Ryushi barely spoke English so he wasn't able to provide much assistance.

Although I was frustrated by my inability to communicate and express myself satisfactorily, I was also excited by the fact that for the first time since I had begun my Japanese learning journey, I finally felt as though I was out in the real world using my Japanese with actual Japanese people.

It was during this homestay that I experienced my first real boost of improvement. The improvement was practically instantaneous, and was almost as though I woke up one day and found that I was suddenly able to speak and understand Japanese on an entirely new level.

I have since had this experience several other times, and have recognized that it is simply part of the learning process. For whatever reason, it seems as though there is some process by which the brain spends a period time incubating all of the new information (Japanese) that the learner takes in. During this time, no apparent progress is visible and it may feel to the learner that he or she has hit a wall in terms of progress, or even regressed some.

However, at some point, this "processing" is completed, resulting in a sudden elevation in both speaking and comprehension ability. I should probably mention here that in most cases, listening ability tends to precede speaking ability. That is, most Japanese language learners will find, at the intermediate-advanced stage, that their ability to comprehend the Japanese that they hear will outpace their ability to produce the same Japanese on their own.

This was indeed the case when I experienced my near-instantaneous boost in ability during my homestay in Nagasaki. Suddenly, everything seemed to click and I was able to understand much of what my hosts were saying, even while my ability to produce Japanese on my own and respond still lagged behind somewhat, although this too had clearly begun to improve.

At Ryushi's home, I enjoyed a traditional Japanese New Year consisting of *o-zoni* (mochi soup), *toshi-koshi* (year-end) soba, and *o-sechi ryori* (artfully arranged boxes of traditional New Year's Day food). We also went to the local temple for *hatsumode* (first temple visit of the New Year).

During my remaining time in Nagasaki, the family took me to the Nagasaki Atomic Bomb Museum and Peace Park, both somber reminders of the atomic bomb tragedy that occurred there a mere 50 years prior during WWII. We also visited Nagasaki's ornately colorful and lively Chinatown. Ryushi introduced me to some of his friends from high school. All in all, it felt incredible to finally have the opportunity to experience so many new places and sights and sounds, all of which gave my Japanese an additional boost. At the end of my homestay, I had made a new good friend as well as a connection with his family. I had finally been accepted on the inside (内) of a Japanese social group.

After saying goodbye to Ryushi and his family, I traveled to nearby Saga Prefecture, where I visited my friend from Ohio State, Nana-san. Nana-san had finished up her year at Ohio State and returned to her teaching position at Saga University, and so when I told her I would be in Kyushu, she urged me to visit.

Aware of my interest in ceramics, Nana-san took me to see famous local Imari and Akita pottery kilns, which I found fascinating. Nana-san seemed genuinely impressed with my Japanese progress, which I gratefully took as a sign that I had made some real improvement.

Nana-san also asked me if I had called the Hirata family in Tokyo. I already mentioned that I met Nana-san's friend Sayoko-san at Ohio State. The summer before I went to Tsukuba, Sayoko-san's sister, Tomoko Hirata-san, came to visit along with her daughter Natsuko. They were there because they had just brought Natsuko's sister Asako to spend a year abroad as a high school exchange student.

During their visit we all had dinner together, and Sayoko-san's sister urged me to call her and come visit once I had settled in at Tsukuba. For whatever reason, probably because I was too intimidated by the prospect of making the phone call, I had neglected to call Hirata-san. When I explained as much to Nana-san, she immediately picked up the phone and called Hirata-san in Tokyo. I spoke to Hirata-san and she again insisted that I visit. I promised that I would as soon as I got the chance.

Grateful to Ryushi and his family as well as to Nana-san, I traveled back to Tsukuba with renewed enthusiasm and motivation, as well as with a newfound confidence in my improving Japanese.

Keys to a Successful Japanese Homestay

Participating in a Japanese homestay is a great way to not only accelerate your Japanese language learning progress, but also to experience daily life in Japan and interact with and hopefully form a close bond with a real Japanese family. However, in order to make your homestay experience a successful one for all the involved participants, here are a few tips you should follow:

Be a willing participant

The most important thing to bring with you to your homestay is an open mind and willingness to participate fully in your experience. This means being open to the foods your family will prepare for you and any cultural experiences that they may introduce you to.

Familiarize yourself with basic Japanese customs

Cross-cultural communication, usually accompanied by language barrier issues, is one of the major challenges of a homestay, and always brings with it the potential for committing cultural blunders and unintentionally offending your hosts. Although your family will likely not expect you to have mastered the nuances of every Japanese custom, at the same time, to most families those same customs are simply accepted ways of doing things and all they really know. Therefore, you should certainly familiarize yourself with the most basic Japanese customs, such as removing your shoes before you enter a home and washing before you enter a bathtub, so as to avoid creating an embarrassing situation.

Make an effort to "be Japanese"

Obviously you are not Japanese, but during your homestay experience you should abide by the "when in Rome" principal and make an effort to embrace Japanese culture and its customs.

Share your own culture

Even while you are participating in your homestay in order to experience Japanese culture firsthand, remember that your homestay family will likely be just as interested in your own culture and background as you are in theirs. Therefore, be sure to bring gifts (*omiyage*) that represent your own background and culture, as this will certainly please your hosts. One friend of mine, during her own homestay, brought taco ingredients and made a taco dinner for her family, which they absolutely loved. Finding unique ways to share your culture with your host will enhance your own homestay experience.

Be open to new experiences

Your hosts may plan activities for you that you are unfamiliar or even uncomfortable with. During my first homestay my family took me to experience karaoke. I was petrified at the idea of singing badly in front of people I hardly knew. But thanks to that initial exposure, today I love karaoke. Likewise, my host family also took me to an onsen. I was initially embarrassed to bathe with complete strangers, but it only took me the one experience to learn what a delightful pleasure a soothing hot springs bath can be.

Make the best of misunderstandings

Despite everyone's best efforts, due to the language barrier and cultural differences, misunderstandings are likely to occur. In these situations, sincere apologies and a sense of humor can go a long way in defusing a potentially uncomfortable situation.

Don't be overly demanding

Remember that during your homestay you are a guest in another person's home, so you should be prepared to orient yourself to your family's routine, rather than vice versa. Often this means leaving the comfort of your own routine behind and living on a different time schedule and daily routine than you may be used to. Self-centeredness is definitely not a Japanese trait, so make an effort to be a willing member of the family group.

Make known any restrictions in advance

If you have any specific dietary or physical restrictions or peculiarities, be sure to inform your host of these in advance of your visit. For example, if you are a vegetarian, be sure to be very specific about informing your host what you can and cannot eat, as you certainly do not want to find yourself at the dinner table rejecting a meal that your host worked hard to prepare for you.

Keep in touch

Following what was hopefully a mutually successful and fulfilling homestay, be sure to stay in touch with your homestay family. Having accepted you into their home, many families will now consider you to be an extension of their own, so cherish and respect your newly formed relationship, which in many cases can mean a valuable relationship and connection in Japan that will last throughout your lifetimes.

Japanese Language Exchange

By the beginning of the New Year, about four months into my stay in Japan, I finally felt that things were beginning to move in the right direction. I had made a great new friend in Ryushi. I had plans to go visit the Hirata family in Tokyo in the near future. I finally had an effective kanji study method that was working for me. And I could finally see real improvement in my Japanese.

One great way to further your Japanese language learning progress is to form a language exchange partnership with a native Japanese speaker, and soon after returning to Tsukuba following my homestay, I met Yuko, a person who would end up being my best friend, conversation partner, and close companion for the rest of my stay at Tsukuba. I first encountered Yuko when she was standing outside of my dorm building. Yuko was studying Japanese linguistics in hopes of becoming a language instructor, and she was trying to corral foreign students to take part in a research survey she was doing.

I don't remember exactly how we ended up talking, but it was clear that she was looking to make foreign friends and was open to meeting new people. We discovered we had a common interest in tennis, and so we made plans to play a game later that week. We enjoyed our game and hit it off, and so started playing tennis together a couple of mornings a week. We also hung out together at a local café, jogged and worked out together, and basically became close friends.

After a while, Yuko and some of her friends expressed an interest in wanting to practice English, and so we formed a little language exchange circle, which began as a group of about six of us, but by the end of the year grew to a group of about 20.

As a result of befriending Yuko, she introduced me to several of her other friends, and before I knew it I had gone, in the span of just a couple months, from never having felt more lonely to having a larger circle of good friends than ever before.

For those of you who plan to live or already are living in Japan with hopes of studying and improving your Japanese, I cannot stress how important it is to do whatever you have to develop a social circle of Japanese friends (who of course are willing to speak Japanese with you), as this will be by far the very best way you can possibly improve your Japanese.

Textbooks and classroom learning are an important part of the learning process, as this will provide you with a solid foundation upon which to further build, but once that foundation is established, your real progress in Japanese will come from actually using your Japanese in real-world settings and communicating on a daily basis with native Japanese speakers.

Arubaito: Improving Japanese on the Job

Although I was receiving a modest monthly stipend from Japan's Ministry of Education during my foreign exchange and didn't necessarily have to work, I felt like I needed a bit of extra cash in order to travel around Japan, and so I ended up working a couple of part-time jobs.

The first of these jobs I found through my friend Yuko, who was also working part time, at a small medical equipment assembly factory. She mentioned that they needed more people and though it didn't pay great, it was actually a lot of fun and that I'd meet new people.

This sounded great to me so I signed right up. Indeed, though the work of assembling little devices was mindless and tedious, it was actually quite fun, as a group of about eight of us sat around a table chatting away while eating Japanese snacks the entire time. Just the ability to sit and converse in Japanese with a variety of people and actually get paid for it was, for me at that time, a dream job, and the positive effect on my Japanese was quite significant.

My second job was teaching English conversation. I got this job by answering a posting on the school library's bulletin board. My student was an employee and researcher at a local pharmaceutical company named Saito. I didn't really want to spend a lot of time speaking English during my time in Japan, but Saito-san was offering 5,000 yen per session twice a week, and so the money was too good to pass up.

Saito-san was typical of a lot of Japanese *sarariman* who venture to learn English: an extremely capable student who had a difficult time expressing himself. The hardest part about teaching Saito-san was actually getting him to speak. During many of our sessions, despite urging him to converse, it would actually be me doing about 90% of the talking. I remember actually developing a sore throat on several occasions as a result of having to talk so much.

I didn't really enjoy teaching English then, and I didn't love my subsequent teaching jobs during my second stay in Japan, but it was for me as it is for many gaijin in Japan one of the easiest ways to make much needed money, and so I bit the bullet and did it. The one positive thing that came out of teaching Saito-san was that he offered to take me on various day trips in exchange for extended English conversation practice. Thus, I traveled with Saito-san to Mashiko in neighboring Tochigi Prefecture, which was a famous pottery village in Japan where my favorite Japanese potter, Shoji Hamada, had lived and worked.

Saito-san also took me to Nikko, also in Tochigi Prefecture, which is famous as the location of the mausoleums of the Tokugawa shoguns and many other UNESCO World Heritage Sites, as well as for its breathtaking wooded mountains, waterfalls, and hiking trails. These excursions with Saito-san were an ever better bargain for me in that he would soon tire of English and for the remainder of the trip we would revert to Japanese.

Based on my own initial work experiences, the best advice I can give you is to find some type of part-time job, even if you are in Japan as a student (especially if you are a student). Even an English-teaching job can often lead to the formation of valuable relationships and friendships, which will in turn improve your quality of life, not to mention your Japanese.

The remainder of my time in Tsukuba was, quite simply, the best time of my life up to that point. Here I was living in the country I always wanted to live in, speaking the language I always wanted to learn, interacting with the people I always wanted to communicate with, and I was actually getting paid to be there! I also traveled. In addition to Nikko and Nagasaki I visited Nara at the peak of Cherry Blossom season. I also climbed Mt. Fuji with my friend Yuko.

Yuko and I decided to do this one night on a whim. We took a bus that arrived at the climbing base of the mountain around 11pm, with the intent to climb throughout the night and see the sunrise from the top of the mountain. However, in our haste, we forgot to check the weather report. Halfway through our climb, it began to pour rain, and dressed only in tee shirts and light windbreakers, by the time we reached the top we were deathly cold and drenched. And to top it all off, once morning arrived it was too cloudy to witness the sunrise, so there was nothing to do but eat a bowl of hot noodles and make our way back down the mountain. The lesson: if you decide to climb Mt. Fuji, check the weather and dress appropriately!

I also finally met up with the Hirata family in Tokyo. The entire family was incredibly welcoming and friendly. The Hirata family lived in what is called a *ni-setai jutaku*, which means a house in which two generations of family live. In this living arrangement, the Hirata family lived on the second floor, while the family's maternal grandparents lived on the first floor. Each floor was a completely separate living space, although they shared a common hallway and staircase, so that either floor was accessible.

This is not an uncommon living arrangement in Japan. The grandparents were also exceedingly warm and welcoming. The grandfather was a retired professor at the prestigious University of Tokyo. Both grandparents have since passed away, and now the daughter, Asako, lives on the top floor with her husband and two daughters while the father and mother have moved downstairs, so it has been interesting to observe the passage of generations within this household.

The Hirata family invited me to their home several times during the year, and became something of a host family to me. I still keep in touch with them and stay with them whenever I visit Tokyo. They also took me to their vacation home in Izu, which is something of a coastal resort town, right at the height of spring when many beautiful flowers are in bloom, as well as to a number of local festivals and attractions in and around Tokyo.

In contrast to just a few months earlier, when I was struggling to comprehend even a word of what Ryushi's father was saying to me, my Japanese progress had shifted into overdrive, and I was finding that I had no trouble spending an entire day with the Hirata family keeping up the conversation entirely in Japanese.

It is said that all good things come to an end, and before I knew it, my year at Tsukuba was drawing to a close. I was having such a good time that it wasn't until the very end of the year that I began thinking about what I was going to do after it was over.

Staying in Japan and teaching English was an option. I didn't really want to teach, but at least it would be a way to remain in Japan. However, it was already too late for me to apply to the JET program, which was the best option at the time for finding a visa sponsor.

I opted instead to return to Ohio State and enroll as a graduate student of Japanese linguistics and language education. Having gone through the unique learning process at OSU and also having had a chance to compare the curriculum at OSU with that of Tsukuba, I developed an interest in studying the theoretical side of the process of teaching the Japanese language. Also, I was so inspired by my teachers at OSU that I thought I might like to become a language teacher in my own right.

I was thankful when I was accepted into the program and also offered a teaching assistantship, which would cover the cost of tuition plus a modest stipend for living expenses. Although in my heart of hearts I didn't want to leave Japan, at the moment I had no other real option to stay and so I returned to the U.S. with the intention of finding a way back to the country as soon as I possibly could.

Kikoku: Life after Japan

It is no exaggeration to say that my year abroad living in Japan changed me forever. I had somehow succeeded in truly immersing myself in the language and culture, so much so that by the time I returned I was somewhat of a poster child for that song by the Vapors "Turning Japanese."

I had used Japanese to the exclusion of English so much that once I was back on U.S. soil, I was actually having difficulty recalling English words. I had also unconsciously adopted many Japanese mannerisms, such as bowing and nodding and using the Japanese versions of "thinking" words like "umm" that we say in English that Japanese use when struggling to recall words in their own language.

I even found myself constantly mixing in Japanese words into English speech, even though my English speaking partners obviously had no idea what I was saying. It took me a while to even realize I was doing these things, and in some cases I had no idea I was until a friend or family member pointed them out to me. And yes, by this time I was actually dreaming in Japanese.

As my plane arrived at Cleveland's Hopkins Airport, I was happy to see my family, but my heart was still in Japan. I had just experienced by far the best, most exciting, most stimulating year of my life, and all of the sudden it was over, and I was back in my mundane, familiar world.

A Quick Lesson on Appropriate Japanese Speech

I had only a few days to visit with my family before it was time to return to Ohio State, this time as a graduate student in Japanese linguistics and language education. Upon my return, my first order of business was to pay an *aisatsu* (greeting) to my professors.

I couldn't wait to impress Noda-sensei with my improved Japanese, and thought I was doing just that when she jolted me back to reality. I had become so accustomed to speaking almost exclusively in the most casual form of Japanese speech with my friends back in Tsukuba that I found myself slipping back into this casual speech pattern even while speaking to my sensei.

However, Noda-sensei, ever the teacher, was having none of it, and whenever I spoke in an inappropriately casual manner to her, she stopped me with a sharp *"Nani?* (what was that!?) and rightfully made me speak to her in language appropriate for a student speaking to a teacher.

There is an important lesson in this little episode. Many foreign learners of Japanese feel uncomfortable using the more polite patterns of speech, particularly the humble polite form of speech that requires the speaker to put oneself in somewhat of a subordinate position to the listener while respecting the "elevated status" of the other party. I know that as a prideful American male, I initially had trouble performing these nuances of speech in class without at least feeling a tinge of resentment at having to do so.

Once at Tsukuba and in a social environment in which it was acceptable to speak in a much more casual style that more closely mirrors the American mindset, I felt freed from the constraints of all of the politeness and formality that Noda-sensei and my other Japanese instructors insisted on drilling into us inside the classroom.

So much so that I began to almost feel as though this casual form of speech was much more "authentic" than the polite forms of speech. In other words, having the ability to speak to my Japanese friends in such a casual manner somehow made me feel as though I was closer to being accepted into the language and the culture. In fact, there were times while at Tsukuba when a Japanese person I was speaking to, even a peer, would insist on using a formal or even an honorific form of speech while speaking to me. This would disappoint me, as to me it meant that they somehow didn't like me or didn't want to get to close to me.

The reality is that *all* of the various formalities and levels of speech are real, authentic Japanese, and the only thing that is important is gauging and using the form of speech that is proper for the social context of each specific situation.

I've already discussed earlier in this book how the various Japanese social orientations are reflected in the Japanese language itself, but I just want to point out through this little episode here that while speaking in the casual style may seem closer to the basic Western style of speech and feel more natural to you, it does not make you "cooler" or your Japanese more authentic.

Rather, if you insist on superimposing your casual Western attitude on a Japanese speaking partner in a social context for which such a style is not appropriate (a teacher, a senior, a customer, or simply someone you do not know well), you will only succeed in offending your counterpart while demonstrating that you have not yet truly mastered Japanese.

Japanese Grad School

After having had this point driven home to me by Noda-sensei, she welcomed me back and wished me good luck in the coming school year. I met my new graduate classmates, most of whom were Japanese, during a weeklong orientation for teaching assistants prior to the start of the fall quarter. During this orientation we were given a crash course on how to properly teach a language class.

Toward the conclusion of the orientation our assignment was to assimilate all we learned and give a teaching demonstration, during which we were required to give a 10-minute demo lesson to TAs of other languages. I still didn't have an official teaching assignment, and I really wanted a language teaching assignment rather than a lecture assignment, so I was determined to impress Noda-sensei, who was in attendance.

I gave a teaching demo on the difference between KORE, SORE, and ARE (this, that, and that over there). I was nervous as hell, but I thought I did an adequate job. I must have, because shortly thereafter Noda-sensei informed me that I had been given an assignment to teach Japanese 101. It was only then that it hit me that I was about to begin teaching material that I myself had only begun learning a mere two years ago.

I took that moment to reflect on the progress I had made in a relatively short period of time. Only a little over two years ago I had just begun my study of Japanese, and could barely put a sentence together. Through a combination of blood, sweat, and yes, tears, as well as an ideal learning environment, I had gained enough competency in the language that the same teacher who was assessing me in Japanese 101 only a year earlier was now deeming me ready to teach the same material.

Indeed, when I compared my current level of Japanese with my level at the outset of my year abroad in Japan, I was struck by the extent to which there was no comparison between the two. After having completed fourth-year Japanese, I felt like I had quite an impressive amount of Japanese under my belt. Then, once I landed in Japan, I realized how much I still had to learn.

Nine months later, I could clearly see how vastly improved I was at the language compared to my first days at Tsukuba. I was no doubt a fluent speaker. My vocabulary was massively expanded compared to my very limited classroom vocabulary. My listening comprehension was in the stratosphere compared to what it had been a year earlier. Back then, I would actually panic every time my conversation partner used even a single word I was unfamiliar with. Now, I felt as though I could understand or at least infer the meaning of the majority of what was being said. And of course, thanks to sticking with my kanji study program my kanji level and overall ability to read Japanese were also through the roof compared to what they had been.

I felt a heavy weight of responsibility at being given an opportunity to teach Japanese 101, and was determined to do a good job, but I also felt as though I had earned the opportunity, as well as the confidence that I would do a good job.

One major concern I had returning to the graduate program was how I would maintain and improve my Japanese now that I was back on U.S. soil. For the first time since I had begun my study of Japanese, I would not be in an immersion environment. I would be learning *about* the Japanese language and how to teach it instead of actually learning the language itself, and these courses would be taught in English, not Japanese.

It helped that most of my fellow grad students were Japanese and were willing to converse with me in their native language. That would help me to at least maintain my current level throughout the year. However, I wanted to do more than stay at the same level: I wanted to improve even further.

The Ultimate Japanese Learning Tool?

Toward the end of my stay in Tsukuba I discovered a Japanese learning resource that had been available to me the entire time without my realizing it: Japanese TV. I did have a small TV in my dorm room, but probably because at first I couldn't really understand any of it, and later because I was so involved in my real-world social life, I had rarely ever turned it on.

Toward the end of my year abroad, a friend of mine, Mayumi, was visiting me in my dorm and asked to turn on the TV because there was this TV drama she was really into. The name of the drama was Long Vacation. I watched it with her, and found that not only did I understand much of the dialog, but that the story itself was quite interesting.

I only had the opportunity to catch a couple of episodes while in Japan before I had to return home, but fortunately there was a little Japanese video rental store near the OSU campus, and I was happy to discover they had a copy of this drama. A video-savvy classmate of mind offered to dub the video, so in no time I had my own copy of Long Vacation.

It is no exaggeration to say that my primary tool for improving my Japanese during the year following my return to the U.S. was this drama. Long Vacation, like most Japanese serial dramas, followed a pretty formulistic storyline contained within 11 one-hour episodes. This particular drama was extremely popular in Japan due to a stellar cast of established and up-and-coming actors, including the now very-famous Kimutaku (Kimura Takuya) and Hirosue Ryoko, just to name a couple.

I became engrossed in the story, but I also recognized the drama's value as a learning tool, and so I probably watched the entire drama at least a dozen times over the following few months. By the end of the year and my 10th time or so watching Long Vacation, I had practically memorized every single line. I discovered that this was a fantastic way to learn Japanese, and I believe memorizing all of the lines in the drama enabled me to get a sense of what increasingly more natural-sounding conversational Japanese felt like.

Although I wasn't a huge fan of anime, the same classmate that dubbed Long Vacation for me was, and urged me to watch a romantic anime series called Marmalade Boy. She made me a copy of this anime and I got into this story and watched it several times over as well.

Today, having lived back in the U.S. for several years now, I still rely heavily on Japanese TV as a source of real Japanese, and watch quite a bit of it in order to stay immersed in the language. Short of actually being in Japan and communicating regularly in the language, once you have completed undergraduate-level Japanese, I cannot recommend watching Japanese TV enough as perhaps your best tool for expanding and improving your language capability.

Teaching Japanese as a Grad Assistant

As a graduate TA at Ohio State, I was now teaching Japanese using the very same system that I had learned under. Although I was very familiar with this system, having been immersed in it only a year earlier, it was certainly a different feeling to be on the opposite side of the podium teaching. Knowing firsthand the quality of Japanese education I had received at this very same institution, I felt a tremendous responsibility and pressure to live up to the program's high standard and deliver that same quality of instruction to my own students.

My initial impression of teaching Japanese is that it was extremely rewarding, but also far more difficult than I imagined. I loved being in the classroom teaching and interacting with the students. Less enjoyable was the laborious preparation and grading in between classes. As a student I had never realized just how much time and effort was required to prepare for a single class.

As a teacher, I did my very best to prepare for and teach each class so as to provide a quality learning experience for my students. I certainly felt that I had sufficient grasp of the material I was teaching to be qualified to be in that position. However, at the same time, as proud as I was at my rapid progress, the fact that I had myself been a Japanese 101 student only a couple brief years ago, along with the fact that I had only so far spent a mere 10 months in Japan, began to gnaw at me. I felt that in order to be a truly qualified teacher, I needed more firsthand experience living in Japan and using the language on a day-to-day basis. As a result, even though I enjoyed teaching, I began to have doubts about settling into a teaching career at this still-early stage of my Japanese development, at least until I spent more extended time living in Japan in order to further experience and gain deeper insight into the culture and the language.

Although I had assumed that my formal classroom study of Japanese was behind me, it turned out that I would be in for one

97

more year of it. After returning to OSU, my goal was to find a way to experience another year abroad as soon as possible. I knew that there were some study abroad opportunities available through the graduate program.

The one that ended up panning out was a year of study at the Stanford Inter-University Center for Japanese Studies in Yokohama, Japan. This institution, administered by Stanford University, is a school located in Yokohama that invites mostly graduate students from some of the best universities in the U.S. who are doing Japan-related research to spend a year focusing on concentrated study of the Japanese language. I wasn't sure if I needed another year of formal Japanese study, but I was sure that I wanted to return to Japan by any means possible, and so I applied and was accepted to this program.

The summer prior to leaving for this program, I took a summer intensive Japanese teacher training seminar at Ohio State. The participants in this program were individuals, all of whom were Japanese and mostly from other institutions, who were interested in getting a crash training course in how to be a Japanese language instructor.

Like the undergraduate summer intensive language programs that I went through as an undergraduate student, the pace of this program was intense, and because we students spent many hours together each day, we quickly formed a close bond.

As the only participant from Ohio State and the only non-Japanese in the program, the other students looked to me to show them around and I was glad to do so. As a result, I ended up spending the entire summer with a great group of Japanese friends. This enabled me to use Japanese exclusively throughout that summer, which resulted in further improvement.

At the end of August, the summer program ended and I said goodbye to a group of individuals who had in a short period of time become great friends. Then it was time to look forward to my second year in Japan.

PART 4:
Advanced Japanese Study

Compared to my first trip to Japan just two years prior, I now felt like an experienced veteran Japan traveler. I was used to the plane flight and confident in my ability to navigate the airport, buses, and the city train lines on my own, and of course I was much more confident in my language ability as well.

Still, there were plenty of unknowns awaiting me as I arrived in Yokohama for my second stay in Japan. What would the school be like? How would I make new friends in a new city? How was my Japanese going to stack up against my classmates', most of whom were brilliant students from Ivy League caliber schools? How was I going to afford the school year?

The first order of business was getting my living arrangements squared away. Unlike at Tsukuba, where I had all of my expenses paid through the generosity of Japan's Ministry of Education, this time I was pretty much on my own. I had managed to secure a scholarship that covered the cost of my tuition, but otherwise I was going to have to find a way to make ends meet. Affording my own apartment was pretty much out of the question, but I found out that two students per year were accepted to live in an employee dormitory of Isuzu Motors, the car manufacturer.

In Japan, many large companies have employee dorms for their young male employees. These dorms presumably foster a sense of closeness among the young employees who will be working together for the next 40 years or so, and also provide them with dirt-cheap living accommodations while they get through their first years at the company working on very modest salaries.

For whatever reason, the school had an arrangement with the company to permit two students to live in the dorm. Since the dorm rent was about 20,000 yen per month (about $180 back then), I jumped at the opportunity. The dorm was actually located quite far from the school in Center Minami, a suburb of Yokohama. In fact, it was about a 40-minute subway ride, plus about another 20 minute walk from the station to the dorm.

Before actually being admitted to the dorm, we had to greet the dorm manager and formally ask his permission to live there. I and the other student accompanied the school's office manager, Tanaka-san, who would be making our introduction, to the dorm. Once we arrived, Tanaka-san formally requested that we be allowed to stay in the dorm. The dorm manager, Ishida, was an older gentleman with a gruff manner and a chain smoking habit. He eyed us coolly and asked us a few questions. Then he appeared to think about it for a while. Finally, he granted his permission, and we were allowed to live in the dorm for the year.

This little episode of formal introduction and asking permission illustrates one of the many rituals of formality one encounters in Japan. In situations like these, it is never a simple, casual manner of just showing up and taking up residence. There must be a formal introduction and request, as well as deference to the individual in charge. Although presumably the outcome was never in doubt, it was still a bit nerve-wracking to have to go through such a process.

My dorm mate from the school was Dave. Dave was an ex-military who had spent a couple years in Japan following his military stint as an English teacher before enrolling in the University of Hawaii to study Japanese literature. In contrast to myself, who was fortunate to have received high-quality, guided linguistic training from the beginning, Dave was mostly self-taught.

Dave's single-minded dedication to his study of Japanese was impressive. He was particularly a whiz at kanji and vocabulary. His study method was to write down kanji and vocabulary words on index cards, and then spend pretty much every waking hour memorizing them. His knowledge of kanji and vocabulary was immense.

However, like Theo from Tsukuba, his actual speech was not very fluent, and perhaps due to a lack of corrective feedback, his pronunciation was quite a bit off, even to my gaijin ears. I bring this up not to belittle Dave's ability, which far outshined mine in other areas of Japanese, but simply to once again illustrate how differences in learning environment can highly influence the development of one's Japanese.

Since I had, particularly at the outset, learned Japanese in an environment where corrective feedback was instantaneous and mandatory, I developed very good pronunciation, so much so that on many an occasion I was mistaken for a native Japanese speaker while on the phone. Likewise, because my Japanese course of study emphasized performance of the spoken language, my actual delivery of Japanese was quite fluent. What I mean by this is that although I certainly didn't know as much Japanese as a native speaker by any means, I had developed the ability to deliver the Japanese I *did* know in a highly fluent and natural sounding manner. On the downside, I had still barely managed to learn all of the Joyo kanji (not having focused on kanji during the previous year), my actual ability to read at a high level was still quite deficient, and my overall vocabulary, while sufficient for day-to-day speech, was still relatively limited.

In contrast to my development, Dave was a reading and kanji machine. Likely, left to his own devices, he focused on the written aspect of the language, and developed reading and writing to a high degree, while not having had access to an environment that facilitated development of the spoken language, thus the result of his relative deficiencies in speaking and pronunciation.

I point out these differences as somewhat of a cautionary tale to beginning learners of Japanese. Your learning environment, particularly at the outset, will highly influence your Japanese

101

development. Therefore, you should ask yourself specifically what areas of Japanese you most want to develop (speaking, reading, listening, writing, etc.) and choose your learning environment carefully and accordingly (to the extent that you have a choice).

Also please be aware that when it comes to learning Japanese, the habits you establish early in your learning process will often stay with you forever. In particular, if you develop poor pronunciation habits early on in your Japanese development, it can often be very difficult to correct these habits. Make sure you study Japanese using some source of audio featuring native speakers in order to train your ear properly, and make sure to learn spoken Japanese in an environment that provides corrective feedback from a native speaker.

With the formal introduction made, I settled into Isuzu dorm life. Basically, I had my own small room consisting of a bed, a dresser, a small fridge, a desk and a TV. There was a common washroom and bathroom on each floor. On the first floor were the common bath and a cafeteria.

I soon discovered that my social experience in the Isuzu dorms would mirror that of my Forrest tennis circle experience. Despite the fact that we were allowed to live in these dorms, from the perspective of the young residents we lived with, we were strangers, foreigners, and individuals who were not employees of Isuzu, all of which added up to us being *soto no hito* (outsiders)!

Once again I found myself on the outside of a social group and unsure with how to deal with it. I had thought that my experience at Forrest was unique. But now it felt like de ja vu all over again. Perhaps if I had a more aggressively outgoing personality I might have more easily made friends with my dorm mates. I've since figured out that it wasn't that these people blatantly disliked me but rather, like my Forrest members they simply had no previous experience dealing for foreigners, and that, coupled with the default *uchi-soto* social orientation of Japanese, resulted in them just simply doing what came naturally and basically pretending that we didn't exist.

Inwardly I groaned at this realization, remembering how difficult it had been to develop a social life at Tsukuba yet understanding how important it was to the quality of my life and my language development to do so. Nevertheless, I would be spending the bulk of my days at school, not the dorm, and my counterparts at Isuzu would likewise be working very long hours at the company, so there wouldn't be much opportunity to socialize with my dorm mates anyway.

There were a couple of other challenges with dorm life. The first was the public bath. Since I had been spoiled at Tsukuba with my own private shower, I had never actually experienced a communal bath, and the prospect of bathing daily with a bunch of people who apparently wanted nothing to do with me was unappealing. I initially solved this problem by getting down to the bath first thing in the morning, and then only showering quickly and getting out of there, rather than soaking in the communal tub with the other residents (I've since learned to enjoy the great pleasure of Japan's *onsen* and *sento* (hot springs and public baths), and now have no problem bathing with complete strangers).

My other issue was food. I was (and still am) primarily a vegetarian who also ate seafood. The cafeteria menu, however, primarily served meat. Although the cafeteria food was inexpensive, I couldn't afford to buy meals that I couldn't actually eat, and so I initially solved this problem by living almost exclusively on prepared foods from the 7-11 convenience store across the street. Additionally, though it was forbidden to cook in our rooms, having no other choice I smuggled salad fixings and rice into my room and began preparing a daily salad as well as rice in the second-hand rice cooker that I bought, as well as oatmeal using a hotpot and instant oats I had shipped from the states. It wasn't ideal living conditions by any means, but it was inexpensive, and I managed to get by.

Japanese Study at the Stanford Center

The first full day of school at the Stanford Center consisted of orientation and testing. There were about 50 students in the class that year. Many of the students were PhD students from prestigious Ivy League schools doing various esoteric Japan-related research projects. There were also a few students from Harvard, Yale and other prestigious business schools and law schools.

Our first task was to stand up and introduce ourselves in Japanese to our fellow students and the school faculty. Naturally, each student was sizing their Japanese ability up against the other students'. I had had an irrational fear that I would be at the bottom of the crop as far as Japanese ability was concerned, but after hearing a few introductions, I was relieved to find that my Japanese was clearly going to stack up favorably against that of the majority of the students.

The fact is that when it comes to learning Japanese, intellect is not a major factor. That is, the only advantage that accomplished students from prestigious universities may have over, say, a community college student, is their highly developed study skills, but even that does not guarantee success in Japanese.

Ultimately, the ability to successfully learn Japanese has little or nothing to do with intellect. The ability to do scientific research, solve complex math problems, and write brilliant theses will not ensure that one will become a successful Japanese speaker.

The process of learning Japanese or any other foreign language is unique, and has much more to do with effort, practice and persistence, proper training and quality of learning environment than it does pure intellect. Thus, my initial sense of being intimidated by being surrounded by a group of presumably more intellectually capable Ivy Leagers was unfounded, at least in terms of Japanese development.

Indeed, we took a series of tests, written and oral, to determine our level of Japanese ability in order to group the students accordingly, and I ended up testing into the school's highest level. My advisor, Aoki-sensei, warned me that my reading level was a bit deficient compared to that of my classmates and that I may struggle in that regard, but that in terms of speaking I was right among the very best in the school.

Naturally I was happy with this evaluation and also quite relieved, but also nervous about whether I would be able to stay up to speed with my more academically gifted fellow advanced classmates.

Formal Advanced Japanese Study

Going into my year at the Stanford Center, I had doubts about the value of continued formal Japanese education at this point in my development. It wasn't that I didn't still have areas to develop. I most certainly did. It was just that at some point in the learning process, it becomes more productive to have the majority of learning and development come from real-world situations, as opposed to formal, organized classroom settings.

This was certainly the case during my year at Tsukuba. Having gone through an intensive four years of Japanese at Ohio State, I had reached the point where I needed to get out in the world and begin using the Japanese that I had learned up to that point. At that stage of my development, further classroom study would have been unproductive overkill.

With the foundation of Japanese I had developed through my formal study at OSU, the "free" year I spent at Tsukuba maximizing my social interactions and actually using Japanese through daily discourse in real world settings enabled me to go from advanced classroom learner to highly fluent speaker in the course of one year.

However, this did not mean that I was a truly advanced and well-rounded user of Japanese. Although I had studied my Joyo kanji, for all intents and purposes I still did not have the ability to read at a level that would enable me to do much of anything practical with the Japanese language out in the real world. Further, as a result of still not being able to read at an advanced level, my vocabulary was still relatively limited, and while I had no trouble at all conversing all day long on "daily life" topics, I still did not have the ability to speak intelligently or lengthily on more abstract or complex subjects.

My year at the Stanford Center filled in these gaps quite nicely. In addition to a year-long kanji study that all students were required to go through (which for me served as a nice review), most of our classes consisted of reading some relatively advanced material and then discussing the material in class with our classmates and instructor. We also had essays to write and speeches to give, and also were given time to work on our own research projects.

My advanced class was small. In addition to myself was Dave, whose kanji and vocabulary prowess propelled him to the top of the class, as well as Todd, from Cornell, who was definitely the most advanced student in our school. There was also Ray, a law student from Yale, Li, a Chinese student who was also very advanced, and Hannah, who was a half-Japanese from Harvard who was already fully bilingual.

Although I felt a sense of accomplishment to have made it into the school's top class with these brilliant students, I also knew that I was going to have to keep working my butt off in order to keep up with my classmates.

My year at Stanford Center was very valuable in terms of providing opportunity to study and practice Japanese at an advanced level. My ability to speak intelligently at a much more abstract level as well as read complicated material improved dramatically.

Like all improvement, however, the process consisted of feeling a great sense of frustration and struggle to process new and increasingly difficult material, which always resulted in a sense

106

of temporary regression, before emerging on the other side of the effort with an improved level of skill.

As a social experience, however, the school was less than fulfilling. Whereas at Tsukuba I was on a huge campus full of mostly Japanese students with whom I had ample opportunity to form relationships, at Stanford Center the school was a cloistered environment consisting entirely of fellow foreigners.

At Tsukuba I had studiously avoided falling into the herd of foreign exchange students who seldom if ever ventured outside of that herd. And indeed, it didn't take long before the gaijin herd mentality surfaced at the Stanford Center as well. Most of the students there simply made no effort to form relationships or use Japanese outside of the school environment, opting instead for the path of least resistance and spending most of their social hours among one another.

Since I had learned the value of Japanese social relationships at Tsukuba in terms of improving my Japanese, not to mention overall quality of my experience in Japan, I didn't want to fall into that trap and so I had to find a way to form a social life with Japanese locals outside of the school environment. I found a means of doing so at a nearby gym.

I was (and still am) a fitness fanatic, and I knew I had to find a gym to work out in. Since I was a former triathlete and my favorite sport was swimming, I really wanted to find a gym with a pool. I found one right by our school. The Stanford Center was located inside the Pacifico-Yokohama building in the up-and-coming Minato Mirai area of Yokohama. This waterfront area was being developed as Yokohama's prime shopping and entertainment area, and was and is a beautiful place that is now a prime destination for locals and foreign tourists alike. Nearby attractions included Queen's Square, a huge shopping and office complex, Cosmo World amusement park with its enormous Ferris wheel, as well as Landmark Tower, which was at the time Japan's tallest building that also featured a highly upscale shopping mall.

A network of tunnels connected all of these buildings leading from the closest train station, Sakuragicho Station, to our school, and so we would usually walk to the train station via this network of buildings. I was happy to discover that Landmark Tower had a gym that also included a pool. However, I was equally dismayed when I saw how expensive this gym was. Marketing itself as an upscale gym with an indoor rooftop pool, the club charged about 12,000 yen per month, well over twice the cost of an average gym in Japan.

Although I could not realistically afford the cost of the gym membership, I reasoned that I couldn't afford to *not* workout and swim, and I further reasoned that the ideal location would save me time commuting to a cheaper but less-convenient gym.

Financially, it was hardly a wise decision, but socially it ended up working out just as I had hoped. The floor area of the club was very small, and so I found myself working out next to the same group of people every day, which made it easy to eventually strike up conversation and form relationships.

Additionally, the gym had a small studio with group classes. One of these classes was a hardcore boot camp fitness class taught by Tanaka-san, a ripped female fitness instructor with a bit of a hip-hop swag. The class looked challenging and fun, so I gave it a try one day and soon became a regular.

As the only gaijin in this class, I suppose I was something of a curiosity to the other members, and soon developed a nice group of gym buddies. The class members invited me to their *bonenkai* (year-end party), after which I became even closer friends with many in the class, as well as with our instructor Tanaka-san. I became friendly with many of the pool regulars as well.

Compared to the initial difficulties of making friends at Tsukuba, perhaps because I was already experienced in such matters, it took much less time to establish a social circle through my gym at Yokohama, and this again illustrates the importance of becoming involved in some sort of social setting or activity as perhaps the best way to form a high-quality social life that will facilitate improvement of your Japanese while in Japan.

With my gym social life established, I now had a nice, productive daily routine. In the morning I would wake, eat breakfast, and walk to the station. I would spend the 40-minute subway ride reviewing my Japanese notes. Then it was morning classes at the Center.

For lunch, we discovered that there was an employee cafeteria at Queen's Square that was also open to non-employees. The food at this cafeteria was priced very reasonably, and the best deal was a salad & pasta combo which allowed diners to pile as much of each as possible on two separate plates.

I and Dave and a few other starving students became objects of amusement for the employee diners as we would create heaping mountains of salad and pasta, so as to fill up cheaply on what would be our primary meal of the day.

Afternoon would be more classes at the Center, and following the end of the school day, I would typically spend a couple of hours at the school's library or computer center studying my Japanese. Then I would head off to the gym to work out and socialize, and also shower and bathe (my solution to the uncomfortable bathing situation at my dorm) before making the long trek home. Once home, I would eat a 7-11 salad, study a bit more, watch some Japanese TV (by this time I was tuned into several more serial dramas), and then collapse exhausted in bed.

Since I had no funds for this year of study, I also knew I needed to find a job. I hooked up with the local YMCA and taught several English classes each week, which gave me just enough money to live on.

Teaching English in Japan

Many English-speaking foreigners look to teaching English conversation as a means of living and working in Japan. When I first arrived in Japan, Japan's bubble economy was still on its last legs, and it was very easy to find jobs teaching English either privately or through a school. These jobs were also quite lucrative, particularly the private gigs. I already mentioned my private Tsukuba lessons that paid a nice 5,000 yen per hour. It was also quite easy to find a small group willing to pay 3,500 yen apiece or so for a one-hour lesson. School jobs weren't quite as lucrative, but they were abundant, and it was a very easy way to make quick money, as well as find a visa sponsor for one's extended stay in Japan.

Today, English teaching jobs are still available in Japan, but they aren't quite as abundant or lucrative. There are a few large English school chains like Aeon that still recruit teachers from abroad, and of course, the JET program is still a great alternative for recent college graduates. However, gone are the days when you could simply fly to Japan on a tourist visa and line up a visa-sponsored teaching gig within a week or two. You can still try that approach, but it is much more of a crapshoot.

What should you expect from an English teaching job? Well this depends upon a number of factors, including whether you are working at a formal school or privately, as well as the type of student you are teaching (young children, housewives, businessmen, etc.).

If you teach through a formal school, you will normally be required to use predetermined textbooks and follow an established curriculum. For most schools, wearing a suit and tie to your teaching engagement is mandatory. Most formal schools also prohibit dating or forming relationships with students. Private classes offer more leeway in terms of dress, the material you use to teach with, as well as relationship-forming. Private classes also typically pay a better hourly wage. Many English teachers line up a teaching position at a formal school for visa sponsorship and a steady salary, and then supplement their income, and in some cases their social lives, with private lessons.

Many would-be English teachers worry that they do not have a teaching background, or that they do not speak any Japanese. Although helpful, a teaching background is not really necessary, and speaking Japanese is neither required nor desired for most standard teaching jobs. Your primary responsibility is to be an English sounding board for your students, and provided you are a native speaker and are able to lead a conversation appropriate for the level of student you are teaching (usually a very rudimentary level of English), you should be good to go.

My own take on teaching English in Japan is that it is, for most English speakers who have no or only limited Japanese ability and no other marketable skills, the easiest way to secure a visa and live and work in Japan. However, there are pitfalls to be aware of. Although some teachers truly enjoy teaching, many quickly tire of the experience. It can be quite boring as well as mentally exhausting to spend every day attempting conversation at what is normally a mind-numbingly simplistic level.

Many Japanese students and classes are not very responsive to lessons. As I illustrated through my experience at Tsukuba with Saito-san, sometimes eliciting conversation can be like pulling teeth. Young children tend to be more responsive while most junior high and high school students would rather be anywhere else but in your class. Company classes can also be a challenge, since the employees are often only in the class because they are required to be. Even when teaching one-on-one classes with working adults who voluntarily signed up for the class and are paying for it with their own money, many will be too shy to speak up even though they are paying good money for their lesson.

I've had classes where the entire hour consisted of almost pleading with my students to open their mouths and utter even a single a word. However, I've also had fun classes where the students, while limited in their ability, were enthusiastic and responsive. The quality of classes and students, and thus, the quality of your teaching experience, can be very hit or miss.

If you are intending to teach English in Japan with the hope of learning Japanese along the way, there is one essential fact of reality you absolutely must be aware of:

Simply living in Japan will not guarantee that you learn the Japanese language!

Many people mistakenly believe that they will somehow learn the Japanese language by the process of osmosis simply by being in Japan and surrounded by Japanese speakers. In fact, nothing could be further from the truth. Particularly if you go to Japan initially with no Japanese background at all, it is entirely possible that you will come out on the other end a year, or even many years, later with no discernible improvement.

The truth of the matter is that if you want to learn Japanese, you will have to work hard at it. Japan is littered with ex-pats and long-time English teachers who have lived in the country for decades but who cannot speak Japanese at all beyond knowing a few vocabulary words that you just can't help knowing once you've been in Japan long enough.

I remember meeting such an individual during my first year in Japan. Through my friend Yuko from Tsukuba I was invited on a camping trip with several people. One of the participants was an English teacher from Tokyo. Within five minutes of meeting him it was clear that he could hardly speak a word of Japanese. When I asked how long he had been in Japan, I was astonished when he said that he had been living there for 14 years!

Many English teachers simply have no desire to learn the language. They are mostly there to party, meet women, and enjoy the unique freedoms and liberties of being a gaijin in Japan. Thus, if you choose to teach English as your means of living in Japan with the intent of learning Japanese, you will need to be careful with what social circles you ultimately fall in with. Seek out like-minded people, make an effort to form relationships with Japanese who are willing to speak Japanese with you, and avoid the strong gravitational pull of the gaijin herd mentality.

Another pitfall of teaching English as your primary job is that since you will be spending most of your waking hours conversing in English, this is time that you will not be able to spend immersing yourself in Japanese. In fact, since the objective of the schools is to facilitate an English environment, at many schools speaking Japanese is forbidden. Certainly in the actual classes using any Japanese at all is usually frowned upon.

Therefore, if your goal in teaching English in Japan is to use your job as a means of improving your Japanese, understand going in that you will have to make a concentrated effort to learn Japanese outside of your work environment. Particularly if you are a beginner, plan on attending a formal Japanese language school. This is important because while many foreigners do learn Japanese through various social relationships, because they have no formal education, they develop what my teacher Noda-sensei described as "abominable fluency."

Sex, Romance and the Japanese Language

Learning Japanese through Romantic Relationships

One way that many foreigners learn the language is by finding a Japanese girlfriend or boyfriend. Indeed, if formal learning is not an option, learning Japanese through a relationship partner is often the surest route to improving one's Japanese.

For most foreigners it is relatively easy to find a Japanese girlfriend or boyfriend. Since Japanese society is quite homogenous, foreigners, particularly non-Asian foreigners (although in recent years many Japanese seem to have developed a particular fascination with their South Korean neighbors), are naturally the object of curiosity to many Japanese.

Japanese people as a whole tend to be quite curious about people from other countries. Combined with the difference in appearance, as a foreigner this can result in you being considered attractive to many Japanese even if you are not necessarily considered attractive in your native country.

There are many ways to meet a potential romantic partner. Among the most common are bars, nightclubs, and Internet dating sites. However, there is one thing you should be cautious of when searching for a romantic partner.

In many cases, the main thing that will be attractive about you from the perspective of your Japanese counterpart will be your native English speaking ability. To a Japanese person, your native English will sound impressive and even exotic. They will therefore see you as much as a means of improving their English as you see them as a means of improving your Japanese.

Often simply speaking English to a would-be partner will be enough to score at least a first date. And as long as you keep the English flowing, you will also likely continue to impress and capture the attention of your Japanese partner. In this sense, when it comes to meeting and dating Japanese members of the opposite sex, not knowing a word of Japanese can actually be quite a big advantage.

In contrast, if you are a relatively advanced Japanese speaker and attempt to initiate a relationship in Japanese, many potential partners actually find this to be a complete turnoff, and your ability to speak Japanese can actually be a distinct disadvantage that can work against you. I can recall more than one encounter with members of the opposite sex where all seemed to be going well, until the conversation language turned to Japanese, and I could literally see the disappointment and immediate disinterest on the face of my partner.

In fact, even during my first date with the person who would eventually become my wife, who spoke no English at the time, within the first 10 minutes of meeting her, because our conversation was entirely in Japanese, she actually blurted out *"tsumaranai!"* (this is boring!) at the fact that we were speaking Japanese instead of English!

Needless to say, if you have hopes of forming a relationship as a means of improving your Japanese language ability, you should limit your search to partners who are willing to accept you as a Japanese speaker, rather than those who view you primarily as a means to bettering their English. Happily for me, my wife ultimately fell into the former category!

Naturally, the primary objective of any healthy relationship should not be limited to just language acquisition. However, when it comes to inter-cultural relationships in Japan, this dynamic of language sensitivity does in fact exist, and it is certainly something to be aware of as it relates to Japanese language learning progress, as well as success in the area of romantic relationships.

Avoiding the Pitfall of Abominable Fluency

Abominable fluency is the phenomenon of a foreign speaker becoming fluent in Japanese primarily by learning Japanese through friends or, more commonly, through their romantic partner, with an almost complete absence of formal training. On one hand, the speaker does become fluent in the language, in that he or she is able to carry on conversation, usually limited to daily life topics, and do so in a manner which to untrained ears sounds fluent.

However, due to lack of corrective feedback on the part of the person from which the Japanese was learned, this "abominable" fluency is often littered with errors of grammar, pronunciation, and usage, such as inappropriate use of gender and formality levels and a lack of awareness of cultural context.

115

I've met many such speakers during my time in Japan, mostly males who learned Japanese from their female romantic partners. It can be quite amusing to listen to these speakers. Often their Japanese will be unnaturally feminine, since they learned by mimicking the female speech of their partners. Usually their speech will be limited to the most casual form of speech, which while fine in the company of close friends, can be wholly inappropriate in most other social situations.

Incidentally, I've observed this same phenomenon here in the U.S. with the English language. Here in San Diego, where I currently live, there are many couples consisting of a Japanese female and American male (mostly American military personnel who met their Japanese partner while stationed in Japan).

Many of these women are abominably fluent in English. That is, having learned English almost exclusively through their husbands, their English tends to sound uncomfortably gruff and masculine and even somewhat "dirty," especially in comparison to their otherwise elegant, educated native Japanese.

Although abominable fluency is certainly a step up, although some may say just barely, from not being able to speak Japanese at all, once developed, abominable fluency can be very difficult to correct.

Therefore, if learning proper Japanese is your goal, I highly encourage you to avoid the trap of abominable fluency by enrolling in a formal language program even if you are already living Japan and even if you have already formed social relationships that provide you with ample opportunity to use your Japanese. At the very least, make sure to find a friend or tutor willing to provide you with corrective feedback, so that you do not fall into bad and hard-to-correct speaking habits.

Begin Study of Japanese in Your Home Country or in Japan?

This discussion of abominable fluency brings to mind a common topic of debate among Japanese language learners: is it better to initially learn Japanese through a formal institution in one's own country or is it better to begin one's study of the language in Japan?

Noda-sensei argued that first learning Japanese in a carefully structured environment away from Japan for at least a year was actually advantageous in that doing so would enable students to develop a proper foundation of grammar, pronunciation and usage along with an understanding of how to use the language in the proper social context, something that is particularly important in the Japanese language. Learning in this way is also less overwhelming, as new Japanese information is imparted only gradually, and in a pedagogically logical progression.

Those on the other side of the argument assert that the ideal way to learn Japanese is via the sink-or-swim total immersion approach. That is, the individual will learn fastest and most naturally simply by immersing oneself in the society and culture of Japan, and begin picking up the language that way.

My own opinion is that there are advantages and disadvantages to both approaches. Highly successful Japanese speakers have emerged from both methods. However, if I had to choose, I would probably err to the side of first learning Japanese in a formal setting at home, and only *then* going to Japan and immersing oneself in the language and culture.

My reasoning for favoring this approach is similar to that of Noda-sensei's. Developing a solid foundation of basic Japanese prior to actually going to Japan will go a long way toward ensuring that you learn at an accelerated pace once you get there. And perhaps more importantly, provided you are receiving quality instruction, learning in a formal setting will ensure that you not only develop a solid foundation of basic Japanese, but that this foundation includes an understanding of how to use the language in its appropriate cultural context.

In contrast, those who go right to Japan without any formal Japanese instruction under their belt are much more likely to either develop poor habits resulting from a lack of corrective feedback, or if they do learn Japanese, their Japanese may be limited to abominable fluency with no proper understanding of how to use the various forms of Japanese in their appropriate social context. Additionally, many such would-be learners go to Japan with the hope and intention of learning Japanese, but once there, due to a lack of structured learning environment, have no idea how to go about the process, become overwhelmed, and either abandon their initial quest and join the gaijin herd, or become disillusioned and leave Japan altogether without having acquired the ability to speak Japanese.

Of course, my opinion is influenced by my own experience. But it is also informed by years of observation of other foreign Japanese speakers, and in my experience and observation, I have, over the better part of two decades now, observed more successful learners who had some formal training than those who had none.

There are certainly exceptions though. Young foreign high school or middle school students who due to a parent's job or other circumstance move to Japan and attend a Japanese school often are able to make significant progress in Japanese after even just one year. Likewise, migrant workers who come to Japan seeking work at higher wages than they can earn in their own country who are immediately immersed in a Japanese-only environment. And even foreign sumo wrestlers, who come to Japan at a young age and enter a sumo stable and become immersed in a Japanese-speaking lifestyle, tend to become highly fluent speakers of Japanese in a relatively short period of time.

The good news is that simply as a matter of convenience, most foreign learners of Japanese fall into the category of those who first begin their study of Japanese in some formal environment prior to going to Japan. The bad news is that beginning your study of Japanese in a formal setting alone is no guarantee of success. Just as many uninitiated learners go to Japan in hopes of learning Japanese only to find that the task of doing so was far more difficult and overwhelming than they had thought, many students who begin their Japanese studies in a formal environment in hopes of learning Japanese likewise drop out upon discovering that learning a foreign language is perhaps not as easy or as glamorous as they had hoped.

I certainly do not want to dissuade you from going to Japan if you have opportunity to do so, even if you do not have any Japanese under your belt. However, I do want you to be aware of the advantages and disadvantages of each approach to learning. Mainly, understand that your Japanese development and acquisition will ultimately be highly influenced by the environment in which you initially learn, so my advice is to be prudent about selecting your Japanese learning environment, to the extent that you have a choice.

If you do go to Japan with little or no Japanese speaking ability, I highly encourage you to enroll in a formal, structured class once you are in Japan so that you can get the feedback and guidance you need to ensure that you learn how to use the Japanese you will pick up through being immersed in the language and culture correctly and appropriately, as well as to accelerate the overall language acquisition process.

The main thing to be aware of is a point I made earlier but which bears repeating once more: simply going to Japan will not ensure that you learn the Japanese language. Immersing yourself in Japanese society and culture alone will not be enough to guarantee your language learning success. Therefore, be aware of this fact going in and be prepared to put forth an effort to learn, and you'll avoid becoming another unfortunate foreigner with high hopes and aspirations who winds up disillusioned and defeated by the Japanese language.

Ultimately though, regardless of the approach you choose (or fall into by circumstance), your success as a Japanese language learner will have as much to do with the effort you put into learning than the environment in which you learn. Your learning environment, particularly at the beginning, is very important. But even being in the world's most optimal environment for acquiring Japanese will be of no use to you if you are not prepared to put forth the effort required to learn the language.

Results of Advanced Formal Study of Japanese

At the end of my year at the Stanford Center, my progress with the Japanese language was apparent. I had continued to put forth the effort in the classroom as our material became progressively more difficult. I continued to review kanji as I became increasingly more comfortable reading and understanding kanji compounds in advanced-level written media, such as newspaper and magazine articles. Likewise I had taken my ability to use spoken Japanese beyond a basic conversational level. Now I was able to speak at length on a wide range of abstract topics, with a much-more developed vocabulary that was in the process of evolving as a result of now having at least a basic functional literacy.

At the same time, as a result of having developed an active social life in Yokohama, I also gave myself plenty of opportunity to use the Japanese I was learning in my formal environment in a real-world setting. Over the course of the year, my gym friends had become real-life friends, some of with whom I still stay in touch with to this day, with whom I not only worked out with, but dined and hung out with outside the gym.

There are two points I would like to stress here in terms of succeeding in acquiring an advanced level of Japanese. The first is the importance of gaining functional literacy in Japanese as a means to advancing not only one's reading ability, but one's spoken vocabulary as well. I mentioned it earlier in this book, but it bears repeating that there is a big difference between the vocabulary of a foreign learner of Japanese who is kanji-capable versus one who is not. Just as a literate English speaker will have a much broader vocabulary than an illiterate speaker, the same is true for Japanese. Being able to read, and actually reading, will provide you with a source for vocabulary that you might not otherwise be able to pick up and comprehend if you only have spoken-language skills.

This is not to say that it is impossible to develop a highly advanced vocabulary without knowing how to read. I'm sure there are plenty of foreign speakers of Japanese lacking reading ability who have developed an advanced vocabulary, perhaps through watching television, or simply as a result of living for many years in the country in an immersive Japanese-speaking environment.

My point here though is that the difficulty of kanji acquisition ultimately creates a solid line of demarcation between those learners who go on to learn their kanji and thus gain the key to literacy, and those who abandon the effort to learn kanji and remain functionally illiterate, thus limiting their vocabulary acquisition and overall language development.

The second point I want to reiterate is the importance of forming a real-world Japanese-based social life outside of your classroom learning. The reality is that when it comes to successfully learning Japanese, it is not an either-or proposition with respect to learning in the classroom or learning Japanese out in the real world. The ideal is a combination of both. Classroom learning will provide you with the basic foundation you need, while active participation in a Japanese-based environment outside of the classroom will reinforce what you have learned while ultimately accelerating your development beyond what is possible through the classroom alone.

At the conclusion of the academic year at Stanford Center, we took the same placement test that we had taken on our very first day at the center, in order to gauge our improvement. As a way of not boasting but rather illustrating the level one can expect to reach through formal advanced Japanese study, following is an excerpt of the evaluation I received at the conclusion of the Stanford Center program:

At the Inter-University Center Mr. Jones first completed a standardized curriculum in Advanced Japanese, and then went on to more specialized work in his own areas of interest including elective courses reading, and project work. All of these were conducted in Japanese and made extensive use of written and / or audio-visual materials in that language. His project work was on Japan's "big bang" market liberalization and its effects on how people will invest their money. His final oral presentation on this subject was well-researched and well-organized, and was delivered in excellent Japanese.

Mr. Jones' current Japanese language skills can be summarized as follows:

- *In Grammar: has excellent command of grammar; makes almost no errors.*

- *In Speaking: can talk about both general and specialized topics in a theoretical and abstract way.*

- *In Listening: can follow not only the details, but also nuances and implications of conversations on both general and specialized topics.*

- *In Reading: can follow not only the details but also nuances and implications of written materials on both general and specialized topics.*

- *In Writing: can write about both general and specialized topics in a theoretical and abstract way.*

My formal Japanese language training had finally come to an end. My Japanese had clearly come a long way since my first day of Japanese 101. In just four years, thanks to an ideal learning environment that I had fallen into mostly by chance, coupled with a lot of hard work and effort on my own part, I had gone from being unable to utter a single word of Japanese or read a single kanji to being a highly advanced reader, writer, speaker, and listener of Japanese.

I recalled talking to a friend about my plans to study and become fluent in Japanese several months before I actually began my learning journey. My friend insisted that learning a language required decades, and was nearly impossible for an adult speaker. Having encountered many similar opinions over the years, I know that is a very commonly held view.

However, if it was possible for me, a Midwesterner of average intelligence and no special talent for learning languages, to go from Japanese "zero" to Japanese "hero" in a mere four years, provided you follow a similar learning progression and are willing to put forth an equal amount of effort, there is absolutely no reason why you cannot do the same.

Karaoke: Singing Your Way to Fluent Japanese

I want to briefly touch on one more tool that is surprisingly useful for Japanese development and actually quite fun as well: karaoke! As you are probably aware, karaoke is huge in Japan. Karaoke, which literally means "empty orchestra," is a form of entertainment whereby participants sing their favorite songs into a microphone along with recorded instrumental accompaniments.

In Japan, the most common way to enjoy karaoke is at "karaoke boxes." These boxes are actually little booths or rooms that accommodate anywhere from 2 to 20 people or more, thus providing an atmosphere of privacy. Today's karaoke systems deliver a library of tens of thousands of songs. As the song plays, the lyrics are displayed on a TV screen, so that the singer can follow along and sing even if he or she hasn't memorized the song.

My first encounter with karaoke was during my homestay in Kyushu, when the family I stayed with took me to a karaoke box. Now up to that time I had never sung anything in my life. Singing Japanese songs was beyond me, as I wasn't familiar with any of them, so I attempted a couple English-language standards. I was terrible. However, I was also impressed by how good all of my Japanese counterparts were, at least to my ears, and I thoroughly enjoyed listening to the Japanese songs they sang, even though I had no idea who the artists where or what the songs were about.

Back at Tsukuba, I asked my friend Yuko to recommend some good Japanese music to listen to and learn. She suggested two bands that were popular at the time: SharanQ and Mr. Children. I promptly went to the CD shop and bought a CD of each artist, and then set about learning their songs.

After a bit of practice, I was ready to give karaoke another try. Yuko also liked karaoke, so we, along with a couple other friends, went to sing. My first attempts at singing in Japanese also were not great, but for me it was great progress simply to have learned the lyrics to a couple of songs and attempted to sing them.

Karaoke became a regular part of my school routine at Tsukuba, and the more I sang, the better I got. I noticed that learning songs forced me to not only carefully study the lyrics, but also to focus on getting the pronunciation just right.

During my school year in Yokohama, I met a classmate, Ivy, who was also a huge karaoke enthusiast, and so we began making weekly excursions to a local karaoke box. As my song repertoire grew, so did my confidence and my singing voice. In fact, I began to notice a weird phenomenon. I was clearly becoming a much better singer in Japanese than I was in English. My friends told me as much, and even to my own ears my Japanese singing sounded good while my English singing always sounded a little "off."

I've since realized that I developed into a good Japanese singer because of the focused effort I required to learn the songs, and the care I put into getting the pronunciation and delivery just right. I came to realize that karaoke was not just fun entertainment, but a useful learning tool as well. Learning to sing karaoke in Japanese requires that you study and learn the lyrics to your song, that you get the pronunciation and delivery just right, and also that you sing the song at the required speed (often much quicker than normal speech). Practicing all of these aspects of singing karaoke in an effort to produce a good singing performance will actually supplement your overall Japanese development quite nicely.

Even if you are not much of a singer, during your time in Japan (or in your own country if you have access) give karaoke a try and make an effort to learn a few Japanese songs. You may find, like I did, that doing so actually helps improve your Japanese, and you may just end up having lots of fun as well. Plus, karaoke is yet another way to spend quality time with native Japanese speakers, thus boosting the quality of your Japanese social life, and in turn, further accelerating your Japanese learning progress.

At the end of my year at the Stanford Inter-University Center, I found myself in the same situation I was in at the end of my year in Tsukuba: I wanted to remain in Japan but I didn't have a clear means of doing so.

My original plan was to return to Ohio State to finish my Masters in Japanese pedagogy. However, after my second year in Japan I had doubts about my desire to become a teacher. Mainly, I felt that even though I had learned an immense amount of Japanese in a short period of time, my knowledge and understanding of Japanese and the Japanese language was still relatively superficial. I felt that what I needed more than anything was to stay longer in Japan and actually begin putting what I had learned to practical use in a daily-life setting within Japan. I therefore made the decision to not return to Ohio State and instead remain in Japan.

Having made this decision, I needed to find a means of actually staying in Japan, which is to say that I needed a job and a visa sponsor. Teaching English was one option, but it was the last thing I wanted to do. I had no particular background in business or IT, and I found myself lacking any marketable skills other than the ability to use Japanese at a high level. Therefore, I did what many others in my predicament did: I explored a career in Japanese translation.

PART 5:
Marketable Japanese – Turning Your Japanese into a Career

A Career in Japanese Translation

My career in Japanese translation got off to a rocky start. With my year at IUC nearing an end and with my visa nearing expiration, I was beginning to panic. I needed to find a job, and I needed to find one quickly. Almost as if by divine intervention, one day the school held a mini job fair, and a former Stanford Center student visited our school on a recruiting mission. He was from a small media company in Tokyo, which just happened to be looking for translators.

After asking him a bit about the company, I wasted no time in preparing and sending off a cover letter and resume, using templates that came bundled into my Apple laptop computer. I was thrilled when I got an enthusiastic response from the head of the company, who wanted to meet me for an interview.

At the interview, everything seemed to go well. Donald, the company owner, told me how impressed he was with my cover letter and my Japanese background. Desperate for a job and not considering it important, I didn't mention the fact that my letter came mainly from a template. He then asked me what type of salary I would be looking for. I asked what he was thinking of offering, and almost fell over when he responded with an offer of about 650,000 yen per year (about $70,000 in those days), as this was far more than I had ever made in my life.

I played it cool, pretended to think about it, and then accepted the offer. Our arrangement was that I would work on a part-time basis during my last few weeks of school before joining the company on a full-time basis. I would be on a three-month trial, but provided everything went well, he would sponsor my visa and I would become a full-time employee.

I was on cloud nine as I went home, thinking that I had finally arrived in the world. My rude awakening came on my first day of work when I was given the task of translating some product website copy for a major Japanese car maker. I discovered that my Japanese, or at least my ability to translate it, was perhaps not as advanced as I thought it was. It took me forever to read through the Japanese text, and I constantly had to look up words I didn't know. This was still before the Internet had evolved, so there was relatively little in the way of online dictionaries and resources.

In addition to my struggle with reading the Japanese, I found that actually trying to translate it and write it in high-quality English was even more difficult. Although I considered myself to be a very good writer, I was so stuck between the original Japanese and how to express it in English that my resulting translation was the worst of both worlds: I either abandoned the original Japanese meaning in order to write a quality English sentence, or I wrote barely grammatically correct English in order to remain faithful to the meaning of the original Japanese.

After several hours of work I had gotten nowhere and realized that I was seriously out of my depth. At length I eventually managed to complete the translation, but the finished product was dismal.

After several similar projects, I sensed that things were not going well. Indeed, toward the end of my three-month trial period, Donald asked to see me privately. I had a sinking feeling in my stomach, which was confirmed when he informed me that he would not be offering me a full-time position, and that today would be my last day.

After saying my goodbyes to the other employees, I felt sick during the train ride home. I had never so utterly failed at anything and had certainly never been fired from any job in my life. I had already told my family that I had lined up this job, and my mother in particular was extremely happy for me. The thought of having to tell them that I had been fired made me feel even sicker.

Even worse was the feeling that despite the fact that I had certainly attained a very high level of Japanese, as a translator I was clearly incompetent, and now I had no idea what I was going to do or how I was going to secure a visa in order to remain in Japan. Moreover, I had already informed Ohio State that I would not be returning for my second year of the master's program, and so I was really in a bad spot.

With no other options, I contacted my former boss at the YMCA English school who had taken a liking to me, and he offered me a full-time position there that would entail various administrative work about half the time, including some translation, and teaching duties the other half. The salary he offered was only a little more than half of what I had been offered at the position I was just let go from, but with no other alternative if I wanted to remain in Japan, I accepted the offer.

Within my first week on the job, I knew I had made a terrible mistake. I hated every aspect of the job, and couldn't bear the thought of spending the next year in that position. I felt like working in an English teaching environment would be the antithesis of my Japanese goals, and it just felt completely wrong to me.

Thankfully, I came across a help-wanted ad for a translator at a Tokyo-based publisher. I submitted my resume, and was invited to perform a trial translation to determine whether or not I had the capability to perform the required work.

Through my failures at my previous job, I did manage to learn a couple of things. I realized that I tended to rush through my translations, and that I mistakenly regarded my first draft as a finished product, when in reality, I needed to rewrite my English copy once I had initially gotten the basic meaning of the original Japanese down on paper and focus on writing high-quality copy. Moreover, I had to be more careful about producing high-quality English. As I was being fired from my previous job, Donald shook his head and said, "I just don't understand it, your cover letter was perfect." I hadn't intended to misrepresent myself, but I also didn't realize that this industry placed such a premium on good English writing. I had thought that all that mattered was that I possessed a high level of Japanese.

It is often said that the value of having failed is that at least you hopefully learn something in the process. Determined not to fail again, I worked for hours on my trial translation, which ironically, was a short article about Japan's auto industry. After drafting an initial translation, I carefully checked my translation against the original word by word and line by line to first ensure that I hadn't skipped anything, and that the meaning of the English matched up with the meaning of the original Japanese.

Then I spent several more hours writing and then rewriting until the copy read like quality, natural sounding English. Finally, I proofread my translation line by line for spelling and grammatical errors. Convinced that there was nothing more I could do to improve my translation, I emailed it off to the company.

I was thrilled when they called me several days later to invite me to an interview. The interview seemed to go well. They said that my test translation was very good, but they still pointed out a couple grammatical errors that I had made in confusing the plural and possessive (such as confusing its and it's). I was aghast that I had made these errors without even realizing it, but at the interview they told me not to worry, but to be careful on the job. I was hired!

As an entry level position, the salary was even lower than the one the YMCA position had offered, but I didn't care. I was going to be getting paid to learn how to translate and to continue developing my Japanese, not to mention the visa that would enable me to legally remain and work in Japan. I eagerly and gratefully accepted the position.

Working in Japan and Using Japanese on the Job

Life as an In-house Japanese Translator

Act Two of my Japanese translation career got off to a much better start than Act One. Unlike my previous position, where the owner Donald had assumed I was already an experienced translator, this company was looking for an entry-level translator, and was willing to provide training. I certainly needed it. The company I worked for, Japan Echo, was an English-language publisher with a focus on Japanese politics, economics, and current affairs. Most of the company's work came from Japan's Ministry of Foreign Affairs, and work ranged from its intellectually heady Japan Echo magazine, which featured translations of articles on Japan's politics, history, and economy by Japan's leading scholars and experts, Press Guide, a monthly English summary of upcoming events in Japan of interest to Japan's foreign press corps, to lighter material like production of the Kids Web Japan and Trends in Japan websites.

The company started me off with some of the lighter material—articles on Japanese pop culture for the Trends in Japan website. The company's production process was extremely systemized. First I would complete a translation. Then a bilingual native Japanese "checker" would read over my translation carefully, looking for omissions or spots where I misunderstood the original meaning. If I made any errors, they would meet with me and we would discuss them. Then I would rewrite the translation based on this feedback and resubmit it. Once this was OK'd, the translation would be submitted to the company's editor, who would read the English version only and then meet with me to suggest changes to improve the English copy. Only once these final changes were approved would the translation be considered complete.

It was tedious work but I was definitely learning a lot. Back in 1998, when I began work at Japan Echo, the Internet had not yet evolved, and it was still practically useless as a research tool. Therefore, whenever I needed to look up something I had to rely on the company's massive collection of physical dictionaries and encyclopedias and even microfilm.

Today, the process of translation is much easier. There is almost no piece of information, however archaic, that cannot be found on the Internet. There are also plenty of very comprehensive online Japanese-English dictionaries readily available, which makes it easy to look up any word, simply by typing in or even copying an unknown word or kanji compound from a Word document and pasting it into the dictionary search field.

The Three Essential Translation Skills

The constant feedback I received on each translation helped me improve not only my Japanese reading comprehension, but of course, my skill as a translator as well. I was learning what it really took to produce a quality translation. Basically, there are three essential key skills required in order to produce a quality translation:

1. Ability to comprehend the source copy (Japanese)

2. Ability to write high-quality target copy (English)

3. Reasonable knowledge about the subject matter

All three of these components are necessary to some degree in order to produce a quality translation. If any of these are missing, this will be reflected in the quality of the finished product. For example, even if your Japanese comprehension level is perfect and you are thoroughly versed in the subject matter of the translation, if you are unable to express that knowledge and comprehension in clear, well-written English that is appropriate for the subject matter at hand, the end product will be less than ideal.

Likewise, even if you are the best writer of English on the planet, if your ability to comprehend the Japanese is lacking, the end product may read superbly, but may in fact be a significant departure from the original meaning.

Finally, even if you have excellent Japanese comprehension and English writing ability, if you do not know anything about the subject on which you are writing, the translation will likely reflect this lack of understanding, which will be readily apparent to the reader of the end product who likely *is* well versed in the subject.

Thus, I discovered that being a translator is not simply a matter of being bilingual. Rather, translation is a unique skill in its own right, which some translators prefer referring to as a craft or art form.

I found that I enjoyed the challenge of translation, and I loved that I was getting paid to learn to translate and improve my Japanese while also reading and learning about a variety of subjects related to Japan. However, I did not enjoy my office work environment. I had never worked in an office before, and I found it extremely constraining to have to sit at a desk all day, every day. Moreover, I found that translating required a tremendous amount of mental energy and concentration, and that at some point in each day my brain simply stopped functioning. As a result, even though I was at the company in body, past a certain point my brain wasn't operating efficiently, and thus, I was not being productive and therefore wasting my own time and the company's.

Moreover, I also learned that by custom, the employees of the company tended to arrive at work late (the company had a "flex time" policy that permitted employees to arrive at work within a two-hour window). Like at many Japanese companies, daily overtime work was taken as a given. I, on the other hand, had always been a morning person who preferred to begin work as early as possible and leave on the early side so that I still had a bit of my day to enjoy. I made it a habit of taking the early train to work, beginning my day at around 7:30 a.m., and then leaving no later than 5:00 p.m. Even though I was putting in a full day's work, since most of the employees who arrived at work after 10:00 would also work until late in the evening, this probably didn't create a great impression on my colleagues and superiors, but I felt I was what I needed to do in order to remain productive.

Additionally, employees would habitually go out to eat for lunch each day, which was both expensive and filling. After lunch, I would be so full and sleepy that I would often sneak off to the bathroom in the afternoon to catch a quick nap in the toilet stall! Of course normally after these lunches I was not at all productive.

As a result of this sedentary office lifestyle, I began to get out of shape, put on weight and could almost feel myself physically aging on a daily basis. I realized that there was no way I could live like this long term, and so I decided to look for another alternative.

The alternative I was considering was to become a freelance translator. While working at my company in-house, I continued to research my industry. I learned that freelance translators tended to earn a lot more money than in-house translators while working fewer hours to do so. Moreover, freelance translators had the freedom to work from the comfort of their own homes, and at the hours of their choosing provided they met their deadlines. This lifestyle of a freelance translator sounded a lot more appealing to me than my current lifestyle as an in-house translator and office drone, and so I resolved to continue work at my current position for a year or so until I gained the experience, and then make the leap and go freelance.

Working as a Freelance Translator

Working as an in-house translator was invaluable to me in terms of enabling me to get the feedback and training I needed to become a competent translator. Though I realized that the life of a *sarariman* was, at the time, not for me, I stuck with my job and focused on learning and improving my ability as a translator. Once I determined that I had enough ability to go solo, I informed the company that I would be leaving.

Since in addition to the translation work performed in-house the company also outsourced work to some of its former employees who had also gone freelance, I hoped that I would be able to secure the same arrangement, and fortunately, I was. From the company's perspective, they had invested time and money in my development, so even if I wasn't going to be working at their company, there was still value in allowing me to continue doing work for them.

Thus, with my first translation "client" secured, I went about setting up shop as a freelancer. Today I work out of a spacious dedicated home office. This was a bit more challenging in Japan given my living arrangement at the time. Once the school year at IUC was complete, I had to move out of the Isuzu dormitory. I definitely wanted to live closer to central downtown Yokohama where there was more going on, but money was going to be a challenge since apartments were expensive and I wasn't making a very good salary.

Renting an Apartment in Japan

In Japan, in addition to a security deposit (called *shikikin* in Japanese), which in many cases is not just a single month but as many as six months' worth of rent, it is also customary to pay an additional "thank you gift" of about three months' rent to the landlord called *reikin*. Although the security deposit is refundable, the *reikin* is not. Also, Japanese apartments are normally completely absent of furnishings or even appliances, and so renting an apartment in Japan can require quite a significant investment. Moreover, at that time and sadly even still true today, most landlords were unwilling to lease apartments to foreigners, at least not without a Japanese guarantor. Today there are more options available for foreign residents, but there are still plenty of apartments in Japan that will be unwilling to rent to you simply due to the fact that you are a gaijin.

Living in a Gaijin House

I didn't have the financial means or a guarantor to rent an apartment in the traditional fashion, so I opted instead to live in a gaijin house. A gaijin house is a kind of rooming home for foreign residents. A typical gaijin house consists of private bedrooms and a shared common kitchen and bathroom/shower. *Reikin* is not normally required, and short-term leases are usually available.

I found a gaijin house in an ideal location in central Yokohama within easy walking distance to the city's top destinations, including Chinatown and Motomachi, a quaint strip of boutique shops and restaurants, as well as a quick train ride to Minato Mirai, where I had attended school. Compared to my dormitory lifestyle in a barren, distant suburb, my new residence was right in the heart of the city. Equally important was that it was only a five-minute walk from the train station, and there was even a little corner grocery store just a couple minutes away.

All of this was the good news. The bad news was that residence was not the cleanest, and the rooms were smaller than any person who has never been to Japan can even imagine. I rented a 4-*Jo* room (*Jo* is a unit of measurement corresponding to the size of a tatami mat used to describe room sizes; a single *Jo* is approximately 1.5 square meters).

This meant that my room was roughly the size of a modest walk-in closet, and it wasn't even the smallest room in the gaijin house. My rent was 60,000 yen per month, which wasn't cheap, but I reasoned that the location and lack of need to pay *reikin* and buy appliances or sign a long-term lease made it worth it.

Another bonus of living at the gaijin house was that in addition to other foreigners, this particular gaijin house also permitted Japanese residents. This enabled me to make friends with a number of the Japanese residents living there.

My room was barely big enough for my futon, a small dresser, and a TV. I managed to additionally squeeze in a tiny desk for my laptop as well as a fax machine and printer, the necessary tools of the trade for being a freelance translator.

Now that I was on my own translating as a freelance translator, I had to find a way to get some business. My former company sent me a reasonable amount of work, at least enough to keep my head above water for a few months. I attempted a few sales calls at several translation agencies in Tokyo and managed to secure a few more sources of work. Before long, I had a steady, albeit modest supply of work and was officially in business as a freelance translator.

I definitely preferred working as a freelance translator compared to working in-house. Now I was able to work the hours of my choosing provided I met my deadlines. Unlike when I was working at the office, when my brain got tired, I could put down my work for a while and go workout, take a walk and get some fresh air, or even take a quick power nap. I could begin my workday as early as I wanted, and I often began translating at 5:00 or 6:00 in the morning, since this is when my brain was most alert and functional. With a much more flexible work schedule, I now had more freedom and time to get back to going to the gym on a daily basis, which was good for both my fitness and my social life.

Working as a freelance translator did have its downside though. Despite the drawbacks of working in an office, at least it was a social environment. There was opportunity to communicate with my coworkers. As a freelancer, on the other hand, I was now working completely alone. Being a freelancer also meant more responsibility. When I was working in-house, as I mentioned previously we had proofreaders and checkers and an editor to make sure the translations were correct, all of whom provided me with feedback that helped me become a better translator.

Now I had no constructive feedback, other than from my clients, who usually just wanted their translations done right the first time. If I messed up a translation, next time they might look elsewhere for a new translator. Therefore, I was now solely responsible for ensuring that the translations I produced were accurate and of high quality, because my very livelihood depended upon it.

All and all though, I loved the freedom that being a freelance translator offered. I was also making considerably more money compared to my in-house job, at least in terms of the hours I was working. A typical rate for a job from a translation agency back then was around 3,500 yen per page. If I was able to get work from a direct client, my rate might be close to double this amount. Once I added it all up, it came out to much more than the very modest 350,000 yen I was making in my full-time entry-level position.

Compared to a little over a year earlier, when I had gotten fired due to being an incompetent translator, I felt that I had again come a long way in a relatively short period of time.

How to Find a Japanese Specialization

At some point in every advanced Japanese learner's development, in order for your Japanese to become useful as a marketable skill it will be necessarily to apply your Japanese to some area of specialization. In other words, even once you become a very advanced user of Japanese, your Japanese won't have any value other than for socializing or consuming media entertainment unless you do something useful with it.

There are plenty of options for specializing. Many people combine their Japanese proficiency with an IT background. Others work in finance. There are some who go on to get a law degree, and many others who work in some area of business, such as sales, marketing, or accounting. Other options include combining Japanese with the sciences, or even becoming a Japanese language teacher or a college professor in Japanese history or some other Japan-related discipline.

There are also many people like myself who develop their Japanese to a high level prior to developing a second area of specialization, and thus end up marketing their Japanese ability as their primary specialization in the form of a professional linguist. However, even if you choose to become a professional linguist and pursue a career in Japanese translation, it will still be necessary to specialize to some degree in one or more areas of knowledge.

Most professional translators make their living as commercial translators rather than as literary translators. Only a very few translators are able to make a living translating novels. The vast majority of translators translate documents in various fields of industry, research and commerce. Broad fields of translation include business, finance, science, computers, automotive, law, economics, and even manga and video games.

In general, it is very difficult, if not impossible, for a translator to become sufficiently knowledgeable in all areas of expertise, and so it becomes a practical necessity to develop one or more areas of specialization. Since I began my translation career at Japan Echo, my initial areas of specialization became pop culture, politics, and economics.

However, I didn't really have a deep inherent interest in politics and economics at the time, and wanted to focus instead on some area of business. When choosing an area of specialization, there are three primary factors to consider:

1. **Your inherent area of interest. What area or areas are you most interested in? What do you specifically want to *do* with your Japanese?**

2. **Your background. What background of knowledge do you bring to the table that you could potentially apply to your translation career?**

3. **Commercial potential. Is there potential to earn an income from your area of interest or background knowledge?**

Some translators with no particular useful background knowledge or inherent area of interest opt to choose their area of specialization based primarily on its commercial potential. For example, patents, finance, and medical/pharmaceutical are three translation fields with high commercial demand. A translator who specializes in one of these fields should be able to find a steady stream of well-paying work. A translator may choose a field such as one of the above simply because of its commercial potential, and hopefully learn to love it later on.

Other translators focus instead on their particular area of interest or background knowledge, and then find a way to earn their living around that focus. For example, Japanese manga and video game enthusiasts will be happy to discover that there is also a market for translation in these areas. These areas may not pay quite as well as, say, finance, but for those who love these fields, the opportunity to translate things they inherently enjoy and get paid for it can easily make up for a lower pay scale.

There are a couple of other important reasons for translators to develop areas of specialization. For one thing, recall that "knowledge of the subject matter" is a requisite for producing a quality translation. If I were to receive a translation job to do in a subject I knew absolutely nothing about, such as pharmaceutical matter, in order to complete a quality translation I would probably have to spend many hours researching the subject at hand in order to fill my gaps of knowledge. Likewise, I would probably be unfamiliar with much of the terminology both in English and in Japanese, which would require even more study time. Even with this inefficient investment in time, the end product is likely to be less than stellar.

The result is that it is highly inefficient and therefore commercially unviable to work in such a manner. A much more efficient and commercially viable approach is to invest time becoming well versed in a particular area of expertise. For example, let's say that we were interested in green technology. We could develop our area of expertise by voraciously reading environmental technology journals and websites in English as well as in Japanese, and studying and familiarizing ourselves with the terminology and lingo used in this area in both languages.

As a result of this effort, we can now market ourselves as a translator specializing in green technology. Potential clients from this field will be happy to provide us with work since they can count on our expertise. From a work standpoint, we will be able to produce higher quality translations at a faster rate, thus boosting our productivity and earnings.

Of course the concept of specializing applies equally beyond translation as well. If you are hoping to use your advanced Japanese language ability as a way of forwarding your career, I highly advise that you develop at least one other area of specialization *along* with your Japanese, which together will likely combine to make you a highly marketable individual.

In my own case, since I initially developed my Japanese ability without an accompanying area of specialization, even once I became a linguist it was necessary for me to further develop an area of specialization. I found one through an unexpected source.

Working for a Japanese Company

One evening, during a social gathering of participants in the boot camp workout class at my gym, I ended up talking with one of the regulars, Mori was a *sarariman* who came to the class each weekend with his wife, and someone I had never spoken to before. As we were taking, he asked me what I was doing in Japan. I told him that I had been a student and now I was working as a freelance translator.

He told me that he worked for a company called the Nomura Research Institute, Japan's largest think tank, and happened to be in charge of translation in his department, and wondered if he could meet with me to discuss how I might be able to help him.

I readily agreed and we met a few days later. During our meeting, he explained that he worked in a department within the company's financial systems division, and that as part of his job he oversaw the translation of the manuals and other documents for a system used widely in Japan's finance industry.

He told me that he was having a hard time getting his staff to produce quality translations, and then showed me a few examples of their work. He was right: the output was beyond terrible. I learned that the work was being performed by a couple native Japanese translators hired through a temp agency.

I explained to Mori-san that in general, it is best that translations from Japanese into English be performed by bilingual native English speakers, rather than vice versa. In the translation world, it is widely accepted that it is highly preferable for a translator to translate from the foreign source language into his or her own native target language. This is because it is far easier to fully comprehend a foreign-language text and produce a quality translation in one's own native language, while it is far more difficult to actually write in a foreign language at a native level.

In other words, as a bilingual American native-English-speaking Japanese-to-English translator, I have the capability of reading a Japanese text and fully or at least nearly fully understanding all the nuances of its meaning. However, even with all of my study and training, I still cannot quite write Japanese on the level of a Japanese native speaker. It is actually very difficult for most people to write at a native level in a foreign language. There are some exceptions, such as many who grew up and were schooled in a fully bilingual environment or a few exceptional people who through sheer effort, hard work and talent are able to write at a native or near-native level.

In general though, the accepted rule of translation is that it is better to translate into one's own native language, rather than vice versa. In Japan, however, this rule is largely ignored. Most likely, ignorance of this rule in Japan came about because there was and probably still is much more demand for translation from Japanese into English than there was supply in the form of qualified native-English-speaking translators able to capably perform the work.

Due to the lack of qualified foreign translators, there was no choice but for native Japanese speakers to attempt to provide the English translations required for Japan's heavily export-reliant economy. Another reason, though, is that even today, there are many Japanese who are still convinced that foreigners are incapable of understanding Japanese, no matter how much a capable bilingual may demonstrate otherwise.

The result of such translation output, however, was and still is usually terrible and borderline comical. Of course the same would be true if the situation was reversed and native English speakers were left with the task of translating English materials into Japanese.

I explained this fact of the translation industry to Mori-san, but he seemed unconvinced. I told him that at the very least, I could help him edit the translations of his Japanese staff and improve the overall quality of the translations.

Since I was now working as a freelancer but was also eager to drum up more business, I made an arrangement with Mori-san to come into his office a couple times a week for a few hours per day and help him improve the quality of his department's translation output. Also, since I was clearly in a favorable negotiating position, I was able to negotiate a very generous hourly wage.

Once on the job, I discovered that the poor translation was only partially a product of the low level of competence on the part of the translators. Another cause was that the subject matter was extremely complex. The original Japanese in the manuals that were being translated was full of archaic terms I had never seen or heard before, which were only ever used in this particular segment of the finance industry.

I quickly realized that I was as out of my depth as my fellow Japanese translators were. In terms of the three fundamentals of quality translation that I outlined earlier, while I now had the ability to write quality English and comprehend Japanese at a high level, I knew nothing about the subject matter at hand and was completely unfamiliar with the terminology used.

Thus began a long process of studying source materials and spending hours having Mori-san explain the industry and the system and how every little detail worked. It felt like Japanese 101 all over again. Out of sheer necessity I began spending more and more hours at the company office, until I was virtually a full-time employee there on top of my freelance work.

It was all good though, because I was developing a grasp of this highly complex material, and slowly but surely, the English translation output was starting to improve. The arrangement we came up with was one similar to what I had at Japan Echo, only now I was not the translator but the editor. Since I was unable to convince Mori-san that he would be better off with native English-speaking translators performing the actual translation work, I had to make do with what we had. Instead, the native-Japanese translators would perform the translation and submit it to me. I would then edit the translation by marking all over their printed output in pencil and red ink, and then give it back to them for correction while discussing with them why there were errors. Normally this would have to be repeated several times before the translators were able to submit an error-free translation.

I wasn't actually translating, but rather, I was editing and overseeing quality control, which put me in a position of becoming highly versed in the subject matter. This work environment was much more stimulating and challenging than my previous work environment, so I didn't mind coming to work as I did before. Plus, due to my unique work arrangement, I still had a reasonable amount of flexibility, not to mention the fact that I was now making more money than I ever had in my life. Most importantly, I was becoming specialized in a high-paying, in-demand area that I was interested in. I had finally evolved into a specialist, and had finally established a viable, well-paying career using my Japanese.

How to Break into the Translation Industry

How does one break into the translation industry? Well, unlike most industries that require specific coursework, qualification exams, and industry-recognized certification, such as bar exams in the law profession or CPA exams in the accounting profession, the translation industry has no such stipulated path to becoming a professional.

Instead, the only qualification one requires to become a professional translator is to demonstrate one's ability to competently perform the work. In other words, provided you have the ability to produce quality translations, chances are good that you can find work in this profession.

There are two basic ways in which one can work as a translator: as an in-house translator working for a company, or as a freelance translator working on one's own. Let's take a look at each of these approaches.

Finding Work as an In-house Translator

For an inexperienced aspiring translator, finding an entry-level, in-house translation job can often be the best option. The advantage of working in-house is that you will likely receive on-the-job training. You will also have access to an abundance of resources, in the form of both human support and reference materials, which will help you boost your knowledge of whatever industry or subject matter you are translating. Most importantly, you will be able to receive the feedback essential to your development as a translator, so that you can strengthen your weaknesses and gradually polish and refine your skill.

There are two basic types of in-house translation positions: an in-house position at a translation agency or an in-house position at a company in a particular industry that requires translation work to be performed. Each of these has advantages and disadvantages in terms of your development as a translator. Translation agencies specialize in translation, so they are tuned into the challenges of the profession and can best offer feedback and help an aspiring translator develop the basic fundamentals of becoming a competent translator. The potential disadvantage of working for a translation agency is that most agencies handle work on a wide range of subjects from numerous clients, and so it may be difficult to acquire the specialized knowledge in one or more subject areas that is critical to becoming an established translator.

Working as an in-house translator for a company within a specific industry has the opposite set of advantages and disadvantages. You will have the opportunity to develop highly specialized knowledge in a particular industry, but in many cases since the company does not specialize in translation, unless it has an established translation department you may not receive feedback particular to developing your fundamentals as a translator.

In most cases, an entry-level in-house translation position will not pay nearly as well as working equivalent hours as a freelance translator, but the feedback and training you will receive and opportunity to develop specialized, industry-specific knowledge will more than make up for the lower wage scale, and so I would highly recommend that aspiring translators begin their translation career in this manner.

Where does one find work as an in-house translator? The best resources are online job-listing sites like Monster.com, Indeed.com, and Daijob.com. On each of these sites you should fine a number of in-house translation job listings. Search around, and you'll likely find a plethora of opportunities to launch your translation career.

Finding Work as a Freelance Translator

Freelance translation work comes from two basic sources: translation agencies, which secure translation work from companies requiring the service and then outsource the work to freelance translators; or direct clients in the form of companies that opt to deal with freelance translators directly instead of working through a translation agency. In order to get started as a freelance translator, you normally need only three things: a resume, an Internet connection, and an opportunity to demonstrate your ability to translate.

The majority of freelance translators receive their work from translation agencies. The benefit of working for an agency is that the agency does all of the sales, marketing and interfacing with the end-user client, so that you can focus solely on the task of translating. Also, since the agency, not you, is the party ultimately responsible for delivering a quality product to the client, many, but not all, agencies do quite a bit of post-translation document processing, thus improving on your effort and ensuring that the delivered product is a good one. Establishing a relationship with a good agency can mean a steady supply of work for years to come.

However, the obvious downside of working for an agency is that since the agency is the middleman in each transaction, they take a generous cut of money the client is paying for the translation, often half or more, and so a freelance translator is essentially wholesaling his or her services in such an arrangement. Moreover, since the workflow from a single agency can be inconsistent, most freelance translators who work primarily through agencies work for several agencies at once, so that there are multiple sources for work.

How do you establish a working relationship with a translation agency? The most common method is to contact them, submit a resume, and then take a translation test. Most agencies have prospective freelances perform a brief translation test, usually unpaid, as the primary means of gauging the prospective translator's ability. Provided you perform well on the test, the agency may begin sending you work, and provided your output is consistently of high quality, the agency may begin sending you a steady supply of work and you may soon find yourself actively on your way to establishing a career as a freelance translator.

Some freelance translators bypass translation agencies altogether and opt instead to work directly for end-user clients. The obvious advantage of such an arrangement is that by cutting out the middleman, the translator can receive the full sum of the fee the client is willing to pay. This means that the freelance translator is now selling his service as a retail product instead of a wholesale product, and so can either earn up to twice as much as a translator working through an agency, or earn the same amount with only half of the volume of output.

While this arrangement may certainly sound preferable, it carries with it far more responsibility. When working for a direct client, the translator, not the agency, is entirely responsible for the quality of the finished product, and so a higher level of performance is normally expected. In addition, the translator is responsible for all of the sales, marketing and customer service that goes into establishing a working relationship with a direct client. Additionally, many large companies have regulations and systems in place that essentially prohibit transacting business with individuals, and so in order to secure direct clients a freelance translator may have to establish and represent him or herself as a business entity rather than an individual, which can involve more cost and complexity than simply working as a single sole proprietor.

Which path to becoming a freelance translator you choose is ultimately up to your own unique set of circumstances and preferences. Many translators prefer to bypass the complexity and responsibility that comes from dealing with direct clients and instead concentrate on their craft by working with translation agencies. Other freelancers may prefer to work for direct clients, but lack confidence in their spoken business Japanese or even their ability to deliver an adequate finished product, and so rely on agencies to do all of the sales, marketing, and post-translation processing.

I have personally worked as a freelance translator for both agencies and direct clients, and far prefer to deal directly with end users. Since I have confidence in my spoken Japanese, I have no issues communicating directly with my clients, and I have enough years of experience under my belt that I have confidence in my ability to deliver quality translations to my clients without relying on a third party to clean up my work. Furthermore, in addition to the higher wages paid my direct clients as a result of eliminating the middleman, I like that as a result of working directly with my end-user clients the subject matter is consistent, thus enabling me to develop a greater depth of knowledge and deliver higher-quality translations. I can also communicate directly with persons in the know within the company when I have questions, resulting in a smoother translation process.

If you want to learn more about a career as a Japanese translator, below are several useful resources:

Japan Association of Translators (JAT) – A Japan-based organization of individual Japanese translators. The JAT website contains many valuable articles and other resources for aspiring translators. Although most JAT members are established translators, it is certainly worthwhile for aspiring translators to join.

Honyaku Mailing List – This is an email list on which working translators discuss issues related to their field. Free to join; lots of good information.

Getting Started as a Translator – Here is a link to a post many years ago from the Honyaku Mailing List that is a collection of advice on how to get started as a Japanese translator. Some of the advice may be a bit outdated, but a good read nonetheless:

Proz – A portal for translators of all languages, contains many resources valuable for a new translator.

PART 6:
Life after Japan and Dealing with Reverse Culture Shock

All too soon, my fourth year of Japan was winding down. I now had a stimulating, well-paying job that I was enjoying while able to use Japanese on a daily basis in a business environment. I had an active, established social life with many Japanese friends. And I even had a steady girlfriend that I had been dating for close to a year. However, I was also at a crossroad. On one hand, I loved Japan and could easily see myself staying there indefinitely, possibly even forever. On the other hand, I wasn't sure if I was ready to make a choice to never return home to live in the U.S. again.

You see, when you immerse yourself in the study of the Japanese language and commit to learning the nuances of the language and culture, you can't help but to undergo something of an identity change. After having spent the better part of the past five years living in Japan and immersed in the language and culture, indeed I felt that I was beginning to undergo a subconscious personality transformation.

Due to my strict training in my Ohio State Japanese classes and my commitment to abide by the "When in Rome, Do as the Romans Do" approach to living in a foreign culture, I had made an effort to studiously learn and follow the linguistic and cultural norms and mannerisms unique to the Japanese and Japanese culture.

For example, I now unconsciously bowed as a Japanese person would in the many occasions throughout the day when such

151

is normally called for. This is in stark contrast to when I was a beginning student, and my prideful American self had resented the idea of bowing to anyone. Likewise, as discussed earlier in the book, the social norms of Japan are imbedded in the language, and it is difficult to use the language properly without at least subconsciously conforming to these social norms. One example is using a humble-polite form of speech toward a person who, at least within Japan's social structure, is of a higher status. After four years of Japan, I was now able to do this without a second thought, and as far as using Japanese properly goes, this is certainly a good thing. However, a secondary result of this was that that mastering this and similar nuances of the language resulted in an unconscious change in my personality, so that I began to accept such social conventions as the norm.

As a result, I began to feel as if I there was a part of me that was literally "turning Japanese." Now, I didn't really have a problem with that per se, particularly in so far as I was actually living in Japan and interacting with the culture and the people on a daily basis, and thoroughly enjoyed doing so. However, at the same time, I began to feel as though I was in danger of losing grasp on my original self-identity as an American. My personality was changing, and I began to be unsure of whether or not this was a good thing.

The company I was now working for pretty much on a full-time basis now offered to have me join the company as a *seishain* (a permanent, full-time salaried employee). Additionally, although I had enjoyed the active social community at the gaijin house where I was living, it was clearly not a long-term living solution, and so I also needed to decide whether to commit to a lease and the considerable resources required to rent an apartment.

After some serious soul searching, I decided that I needed to move back to the U.S. and gain a distanced perspective on my experience in Japan before committing to living there for the long-term. I had to figure out for myself whether I truly was going to be happy not only living in Japan but being OK with my subconscious personality transformation, or whether I wanted to hang on to my American identity, the person I regarded as being the real "me."

I also had a time-sensitive childhood dream beyond the scope of this book that I wanted to pursue, which would have been difficult to do in Japan, and so after a great deal of internal debate, I decided to move back to the U.S. at the end of 2000 and relocate to the West Coast.

It was with mixed feelings and a heavy heart that I said my goodbyes to my fellow company employees and all of the many amazing friends that I made during my stay in Japan. A part of me never wanted to leave, but I convinced myself that I was doing the right thing.

I physically settled into my new life in San Diego, California in January 2001, but emotionally my heart remained in Japan for many months thereafter. In fact, now more than 10 years later I can honestly say that there is a part of me that remains emotionally attached to Japan.

There is no doubt that my relatively brief time living in Japan had changed me and altered my way of thinking and even my very belief system. A person who has never lived abroad only has a single point of reference for their underlying belief system and view of the world, formed and defined by the only culture in which they have grown up and lived. However, if you live for an extended period of time in a culture that has significantly different customs and ways of approaching daily life and interacting with one another, it is only natural that your own belief system will be affected by your experience. Once you are aware of the existence of and have experienced firsthand alternative ways of thinking, living and interacting that are at a departure from those you have grown up with believing to be the only way of doing things, the result can be a significant change in one's own belief system and view of the world.

During my time in Japan I certainly found that there were many Japanese ways of doing things that were unique to me when I first encountered them, but which as I grew accustomed to I found that I actually preferred. For example, Japanese people are universally regarded as being exceedingly polite. Now, in Japan there is a concept called *honne* and *tatemae* (本音 & 建前). This refers to the distinction between a Japanese person's true inner feelings and emotions (本音) and the actual feelings and behaviors that person shows outwardly (建前).

Whereas in many cultures it is accepted as normal to express one's true feelings outwardly, in Japan the norm is to maintain an outward projection of calm and imperturbability regardless of what one is actually feeling or thinking inside. Now, it is certainly reasonable to debate whether this practice is a healthy and desirable one. There are certainly some drawbacks to this social orientation, at least from the perspective of an uninitiated foreigner, as this practice presents ample opportunity for misunderstanding.

Among Japanese, even while everyone may interact with their *tatemae* face on, Japanese people are also normally very keyed in on the subtleties of social interaction and are able to pick up clues as to their counterparts' *honne* even while offering no real outer hint of having done so, since they too are practicing *tatemae*. A full discussion of this aspect of Japanese culture and social interaction is beyond the scope of this book, but it certainly is a very real phenomenon that foreign learners of Japanese are sure to encounter sooner or later, and will eventually have to negotiate as part of their participation in Japanese culture.

I certainly have made my share of blunders in misinterpreting *tatemae* for *honne*, and vice versa, but in terms of this custom's overall effect on society as a whole, I rather came to appreciate it for the way it seemed to serve as the lubricant that enables a densely populated nation to function so smoothly, with very little visible evidence of outer conflict. I think that most foreigners who visit

Japan are able to observe and sense the pervasive outer calm of society as a whole.

The result of lengthy immersion in this and many other similar uniquely Japanese customs that make up the fabric of Japanese culture and society, for me, and for many individuals who reside for an extended time in Japan or any other foreign culture, was a severe case of reverse culture shock upon my return home. Despite the fact that I was American, upon my return I felt as though I was in a foreign country and found myself easily annoyed by many normal American ways of doing things that used to be matter of fact but which now seemed completely wrong for me, and I began to desperately long for Japan and its culture instead.

For example, in Japan, even in places like gas stations, fast food restaurants and convenience stores, absolutely impeccable, attentive, ultra-polite customer service is the norm. However, when I visited these same types of institutions back home, I found myself appalled by what I now perceived to be a relative inattentiveness and general rudeness of sales clerks and others in service-providing positions.

I knew that it was me, not everyone, else that was the problem. America is America, and there are American ways of doing things that are different from the Japanese way of doing things. But that part of me that had "turned Japanese" was now very much a part of who I had become, and every corner I turned, I found myself longing for the Japanese way and loathing the American way of doing things.

My extended stay in Japan had also affected how I related to other people. I found that my personality had changed such that it was now difficult for me to relate to other Americans, who I now snobbishly believed to have narrow-minded attitudes toward life that I just couldn't mesh with, even while knowing deep down that it was me who was the oddball.

155

Unable to cope with the very American society I had returned to, I sought solace by forming a Japanese social life back in the States. I met and made friends with several Japanese, from which my social circle grew, to the point where despite the fact that I was living in the U.S., pretty much all of the people I communicated with and associated with on a daily basis were Japanese.

For work, I had arranged with the company I had been working for to continue the work I was doing for them back home, and so I was now basically a freelance translator again. As a result, both my work hours and social hours continued to be an environment of relative Japanese immersion.

Originally I had no fears of forgetting my Japanese. By the time I returned home my Japanese level was developed to the point that it seemed inconceivable that at least maintaining my existing level of Japanese would be an issue for a very long time. Even so, the social life I had developed within the local Japanese community, coupled with my work, served as a convenient buffer to ensure that I maintained the Japanese ability I had worked so hard to acquire.

As the months passed, I gradually re-acclimated myself to American culture and society. I began to rediscover my American identity and become better able to relate to my fellow Americans again, to the point where I am much better able to switch between my Japanese-speaking personality when I am interacting with Japanese and my English-speaking personality when I am interacting in my native language.

Still, my four years in Japan had, for better or for worse, clearly changed me forever. I was obviously not Japanese, but neither was I the naïve Midwesterner who had an inspiration to study Japanese and one day visit Japan. I had become something of a hybrid of both cultures. I remain so to this day, and I have grown to accept and even rather appreciate this hybrid version of myself.

Maintaining and Improving Japanese Post-Japan

A challenge faced by many dedicated Japanese language learners who have invested a considerable amount of time learning Japanese as well as a lengthy stretch of time living in Japan is how to maintain and even improve one's Japanese even after returning to home soil.

I've already written about how, driven primarily by reverse culture shock rather than a conscious desire to maintain or improve my Japanese, I formed an active and almost insulated Japanese social life upon my return to the U.S. However, as the years have passed there is no doubt that the Japanese relationships I have formed have absolutely helped me maintain my Japanese even away from Japan and away from formal Japanese language training.

It has now been over 10 years since I last lived in Japan. There is no doubt that my Japanese has grown a bit rusty over that time, particularly in the last couple years or so. My Japanese today feels to me like the engine of an old car on a cold winter morning. It takes a couple minutes or so to get warmed up, but once it is back on the road, it runs practically as well as it did when it was brand new.

In terms of my Japanese level today compared to when it was at its peak at the time I returned home from Japan, I would say that simply through disuse (at least relative to using it all day every day while I was in Japan), my "delivery" is not quite as smooth as it used to be. There are also times now when I struggle to recall and produce a specific word that years ago would have immediately popped up.

As I already mentioned, my kanji handwriting ability has also suffered considerably as a result of now being almost totally reliant on word processing for all of my writing. This is certainly not unique to me. Many of my Japanese friends, particularly those who live abroad but even many who still live in Japan, often complain about forgetting how to write kanji by hand because they only ever do so anymore using a computer or thumbing text messages on a smartphone.

On the plus side, however, because I have continued to read Japanese actively and use Japanese in my work as a translator, I would say that my reading comprehension level and vocabulary of words and terms I can read and recognize has improved significantly. Likewise, because I have made it a point to voraciously watch Japanese TV, particularly the news but also a variety of dramas and documentaries as well as comedy shows and movies, I believe my listening comprehension ability, particularly in terms of the range of Japanese that I can understand, has actually improved over the years.

The biggest difference between my Japanese now and when I was living in Japan is the amount of time I actually spend speaking to it and listening to it. Despite the effort I have made to create something of a mini-immersion environment back home, my Japanese-speaking environment back in the U.S. cannot even hope to compare with that when actually living in Japan, and so it is predictable that my spoken Japanese will suffer as a result.

Even though my daily Japanese remains a bit on the rusty side through relative disuse, there is no doubt in my mind that were I to return to Japan to live, my Japanese would revert to its original level within a matter of months.

In fact, I make it a point to travel back to Japan almost every year, and a few years ago I was working on a project that required me to stay in Japan for about six weeks. Even over this brief stretch of time, by the time I returned home I felt as though my fluency and delivery had returned to its former peak level.

Marriage to a Japanese Spouse

It would be negligent of me if I did not also mention one other important way in which I maintain my Japanese: through interaction with my wife. The girl I began dating while I lived in Yokohama became my lovely wife, and we got married a couple years after I moved back to the U.S.

158

When we initially met in Japan, my wife did not speak any English, and although she may have initially had hopes of meeting a gaijin who would lead her to the English Promised Land, she was in for disappointment when she found that I was quite fluent in Japanese.

I guess she found some redeeming quality in me beyond my native English ability, because we continued dating and I never had any desire or intention, at least while in Japan, to serve as her English instructor, and so our only language of communication while we were dating in Japan was Japanese.

Once we got married and my wife came to the U.S. to live with me, things changed a bit. On one hand, she still didn't speak a word of English and so the most comfortable and efficient language of communication was still Japanese. This was obviously fine by me in terms of being helpful for maintaining my own Japanese. On the other hand, however, as long as we were living in the U.S. my wife was now going to have to make her way here using English, and so I thought it was important that she learn English, and that I help her do so.

The result over the years has been a sort of hybrid form of communication. My wife's first order of business was to attend English language classes at a local college. Since she was less driven and motivated to master English in the same single-minded fashion that I was with Japanese, her progress in English was quite a bit slower than mine in Japanese when I was at an equivalent level. In some ways it probably didn't help her that I was a fluent Japanese speaker, since we would always revert back to that language by default. In comparison, the wives of other similarly composed couples, of which there were quite a few here in San Diego, but who had a husband that did not speak Japanese, had the benefit of being solely reliant on English from the get go.

On the other hand, because I had just gone through an intensive process of learning Japanese, I was aware of and sympathetic to the difficulties of the learning process, and was able to help my wife learn English by providing her immediate feedback and correcting her errors, just as I had received correction and feedback when I was a beginning Japanese learner. As a result, I would argue that even while my wife's English was still limited, her pronunciation, grammar and usage were often better than that of her counterparts with English-only husbands who had no awareness of the language-learning process as I did and so neglected to provide any corrective feedback. As a result, many of these Japanese wives ended up developing the same type of abominable fluency that I saw so many foreign learners in Japan develop.

As for my wife and I, we developed what I believe was and is a healthy balance between Japanese and English. While her English skills were still very limited, simply as a matter of practicality Japanese was our dominant language of communication, although I continued to provide corrective feedback and support. There was a stretch of time when I felt like she wasn't improving fast enough that I instituted an "English only" policy in our household in an effort to force her to use English more. However, this really didn't work, as when it comes to a husband-and-wife relationship, we both discovered that the ability to communicate easily and efficiently takes precedence over the pursuit of second-language acquisition.

However, as my wife's English has improved primarily through her own efforts, she has become able to produce better English in the natural flow of conversation, and so I am always happy to simply "go with the flow" and speak English when our conversation has shifted to that language.

Now close to 10 years later since my wife moved to the U.S., her English is actually quite good, and since she now uses the language quite a bit in her own daily life outside the home, today we tend to speak Japanese at home just so I can stay immersed in the language.

Protecting Your Japanese Investment: Use it or Lose It

Hopefully this illustration of my own post-Japan experience will give you a sense of the type of effort and environment required to maintain, much less improve, your own Japanese on home soil. It really comes down to the tried-but true saying: Use it or Lose it!

Once you have returned home after living abroad in Japan, or once you have completed your formal Japanese language education, you simply must find a way to remain in contact with and ideally at least semi-immersed in the language if you want to protect the investment in your time and energy and even money spent acquiring your ability to speak, read, write, and comprehend Japanese. There are several additional good ways to help accomplish this.

Find a Japanese Job

Perhaps the best way to go about maintaining and even improving your Japanese on home soil is to find a job at which you use Japanese on a daily basis. I do this through my work as a Japanese translator and interpreter. I spend a generous portion of each day reading and translating Japanese, interpreting Japanese, writing emails in Japanese, speaking to Japanese clients on the phone or in person, and most recently, teaching Japanese at a local community college. These work-related tasks naturally have helped me to maintain and even improve my Japanese over the years I've been away from Japan.

There are plenty of job opportunities available outside of Japan that provide an opportunity to use the Japanese you have learned. Following are just a few online resources that can hopefully find a Japanese job that is right for you.

Monster.com

Indeed.com

Daijob.com

Japanesejobs.com

Make Japanese Friends

If you have the opportunity to make Japanese friends, by all means do so. In San Diego, where I live, there is a large Japanese population, which has made it relatively easy to make Japanese friends. However, if you do make friends with Japanese in your home country, you should be mindful of the fact that depending upon their reason for being here, they may have just as strong a desire to learn and use English in your country as you did Japanese when you were living in Japan (if in fact you did live in Japan).

Therefore, a common healthy arrangement with Japanese friends is some sort of language exchange. Be generously willing to help your Japanese friends improve their English, and you will find most of them will be glad to help you with your Japanese as well.

Find a Language Exchange Partner

Even if you don't have an immediate means of making Japanese friends, another way to maintain your Japanese is to find a Japanese language exchange partner. In a typical formal language exchange arrangement, you spend half of your allotted time speaking Japanese, and the other half speaking English (or other native language). An added benefit of a language exchange arrangement is that these often evolve into real friendships.

Hire a Japanese Tutor

If you are at a stage in your Japanese development that you feel there are areas in which you are still weak (and there's always something more to learn), consider hiring a tutor to specifically target and provide feedback on your areas of weakness. For instance, even if your conversational Japanese is solid, you may need work developing your business Japanese. A paid tutor can help you take your Japanese to the next level. School bulletin boards are a great place to advertise for a tutor or language exchange partner. Following are just a few resources where you can find a Japanese tutor either locally or online:

Verbalplanet.com

kakehashijapan.com

Wyzant.com

Find a Japanese Relationship Partner

The same rules that apply to making Japanese friends apply to finding a Japanese girlfriend or boyfriend. It is up to you to find your comfort level with respect to the language in which you communicate, but there is no denying the fact that purely as a means of helping you maintain and improve your Japanese while living outside of Japan, having a Japanese relationship partner can be very helpful.

However, I would like to caution you against forming a relationship with your romantic partner or spouse with the sole intent of using that person as a sounding board for your Japanese. I know of several couples consisting of a Japanese-speaking American male and his Japanese wife in which the man considers it almost an affront to his very manhood to even consider ever speaking a word of English to his wife. Although this militant approach to Japanese speaking may be advantageous for such individuals' Japanese, in some cases it may be not the best thing for fostering balanced, healthy long-term relationships. Of course if your partner is completely OK with only ever using Japanese, then by all means do so. Just have empathy for your partner's language needs as he or she does yours.

Read Japanese Voraciously

Even if you are not living in Japan you can still read in Japanese. In San Diego I am blessed with an enormous Book Off (a Japanese used bookstore chain) nearby, which makes it easy to acquire Japanese reading material. Before this bookstore opened, I would occasionally drive up to the store's Orange County location in search of reading material. Likewise, whenever I visit Japan, I make sure to stock up on Japanese books and magazines. Even if you do not have access to resources like these, you can always order Japanese books from Amazon Japan, and of course, the Internet is right at your fingertips with Japanese websites to read on every conceivable subject.

Watch Japanese TV

Although "watch TV" is generally not the best life advice, when it comes to language acquisition and maintenance, there is perhaps no better tool outside of direct communication. Many cable TV packages include an option for TV Japan or a similar Japanese programming station. In San Diego, where I live, there are a couple of Japanese video stores. Even if these resources are not available to you, Netflix has a decent selection of Japanese movies, and there is an endless supply Japanese video you can watch on the Internet on YouTube or other similar sites.

The above are just some of the methods I have used and continue to use over the years to stay as immersed in Japanese as possible now that I am living outside of Japan.

Full Circle: Teaching Japanese

In 2008, the global economy collapsed, which also hurt Japan's economy, and my translation business suffered some as a result. I therefore found myself seeking a means of supplementing my income when a friend told me about a job opening at a local community college for a part-time Japanese teacher.

Since translation business was slow and I was eager for a new challenge, I applied for the job and was hired soon after. It had been well over ten years since I had last formally taught Japanese while I was a graduate student at Ohio State, but I was excited for the opportunity.

Having worked as a professional Japanese linguist and having learned Japanese through formal education, I felt I had reached a stage in my life and in my Japanese language development where I could now effectively share my experience both as a lifelong Japanese learner and as a professional linguist.

The first class I was assigned to teach was Japanese 101, and I couldn't have been happier with this assignment. For one thing, I was unfamiliar with the textbook used at the college (Genki Japanese), and so it was ideal for me to progressively teach my way through the textbook from the beginning so I had a firm grasp on what material my students had covered. More importantly, I believe that Japanese 101 is the most important class that a Japanese learner ever takes, as this class sets the foundation for all subsequent learning, both in terms of establishing the basic foundation of the language and also the habits and way of approaching Japanese study which to a large degree is highly influenced by that first class. In fact, I remember my own professor Noda-sensei telling us that if she was going to choose any single class to teach (rather than delegate to other instructors), it would be Japanese 101 for just those reasons.

I believed that based on my own learning experiences at three separate well-regarded institutions for Japanese study, I had a good understanding of not only what beginning Japanese learners need to learn, but more importantly, *how* they should ideally approach their study and the types of language learning habits that were essential to form from the very beginning.

Since the class I was teaching met only twice per week for 2.5 hours per class, I divided the class into two parts: a "Japanese only" portion of the class where students would be expected to perform their Japanese in class and demonstrate their grasp of the material studied up to that point; and a lecture portion toward the end of the class during which students would be free to ask questions in English *about* the Japanese they were studying.

All the teachers of Japanese 101 were required to cover the same amount of material: the first five chapters of the textbook, plus introduce hiragana, katakana, and over 100 kanji, but at this institution, how we taught and how we graded was left to the discretion of each teacher.

Drawing on the "daily grade" system used at Ohio State, I developed my own version that I believed was appropriate for my particular class. Basically, I gave a daily grade based on four basic criteria: attendance, preparation, participation, and performance, with each of these criteria being worth an equal portion of the daily grade.

Compared to the daily grade system used when I was a student at OSU, which was based solely on performance, my own system is perhaps rather generous by comparison. However, there was reasoning behind my approach. My goal in teaching Japanese 101 was not only to get the students to learn and be able to actually perform the material, but to develop the precise study habits that I believe to be essential to language-learning success.

In my opinion, the four basic habits essential to Japanese language learning success (and any other language) both inside the classroom and beyond are embodied in this daily grade criteria:

The Four Learning Habits

Attendance: the most successful language learners are those who actually attend class on a regular basis. There are other types of classes in which one can get by without being present in class, simply by cramming the material before a test. I once got through a biology lecture class in this way. I figured out that the tests were simply based on the chapters we were assigned to read, and so since I wasn't particularly interested in the class content, and was only taking it because it was required, I simply crammed the day before each test and managed a decent passing grade. Japanese learning, in contrast, just doesn't work this way. Class is where you have an opportunity to actually use and perform the Japanese you study away from class and receive the feedback essential to learning. In my experience as both a learner and a teacher, those students with poor attendance invariably fall behind and eventually drop out. Therefore, as basic as it may sound, attendance is a fundamental criterion for language learning success in the classroom. Even beyond the classroom the corollary to Attendance is consistency of effort, or adherence to the maxim: 99% of success is showing up!

Preparation: attending class is important, but actually coming to class having prepared for each day's lesson by doing all of the assigned homework and drills is even more important. Material usually comes fast and furiously in Japanese 101 as well as all classes thereafter. The material you learn in the beginning serves as the foundation for the material that comes later. If you do not give your due attention to fully studying and practicing the material at hand, at some point you will find yourself unable to grasp more complex material due to a weakness in your foundation. Therefore, attentively preparing for each and every lesson is essential to successful Japanese language learning. Here too, consistency is key. Outside the classroom, the corollary to preparation is thoroughness of study. Don't just gloss over whatever Japanese you happen to be studying; keep working until you "own" the material you are currently working on.

Participation: in every Japanese class I have either taken or taught, there always are a few students who eagerly seek to participate in class at every opportunity, as well as a number who do everything they can to remain invisible and silent. Japanese students who aggressively participate almost invariably outperform those who studiously avoid participation. Some students shy away from participating because they are afraid they will "lose points" if their performance is off and that participating more actively will be a disadvantage in terms of their grade. However, teachers should recognize and reward active participation, as long as it is backed by proper preparation, and in the long run, active participation in class will go a long way toward a student's success as a Japanese language learner. Participation in Japanese beyond the classroom means being proactive in forming Japanese-speaking relationships and creating your own opportunities to use Japanese as much as possible.

Performance: finally, actual performance, or practice, of the Japanese being learned is essential for successful language acquisition. Different teachers and different institutions employ different approaches to learning, and not all teachers and not all curriculums emphasize actual performance in class. Many classes are taught in "open-book fashion" and student grades are based primarily on multiple-choice tests, with no evaluation based on whether the student has actually processed and can perform the Japanese at hand. However, if students are not held accountable in some manner in the class for actually demonstrating their grasp of the material and the ability to perform it, even if they end up with an "A" in the class it doesn't necessarily mean that they have mastered the material. When it comes to Japanese, what you can do with the language is far more valuable than what you know about the language.

Today, when I am standing in front of my class teaching Japanese 101, I feel like I can see myself from 20 years ago, an eager student embarking on the very start of what will be a long and challenging and hopefully unimaginably rewarding journey. I know that in any given class, only a small handful of students will persist through the school's entire Japanese curriculum, and of these, perhaps only one or two will continue their Japanese journey beyond the classroom to become fluent and gain a level of mastery over this language, and with it, the key to the Japanese culture.

I know from my own personal experience how incredibly rewarding learning Japanese can be, and I am thankful that I was somehow able to persist through my earliest struggles to eventually gain my own measure of mastery over the language, and with it, the key to the countless experiences that have shaped my adult life and made it more rewarding than I ever could have imagined.

I wrote How to Master Japanese to hopefully inspire those at the outset of or midway through their own language learning journey to persist through the struggles and stay on the path, because I can promise you the effort will be worth it. If just one reader who may have otherwise given up stays the course as a result of reading this book and goes on to master Japanese in their own right, then the effort I put into writing it will have been more than worth it. Ganbatte Kudasai!!!

EPILOGUE:
Going Back Home to Japan

Over a decade ago, I made a decision to move away from Japan and back to the U.S., unsure if I was ready to "turn Japanese" and abandon not only the country and culture in which I was born and raised, but a large chunk of my American identity as well. After 12 years back in the U.S., I've come to a realization: I've been homesick. Although I am an American and will never and don't necessarily aspire to fully "turn Japanese," I've come to realize that home is where the heart is, and for me, my heart is in Japan, my adopted country and culture. As a result, my wife and I have decided to move back to Japan.

After living in the U.S. for the past 12 years, I believe I have the answer to my question of whether or not I would be OK living out the rest of my years in Japan. The answer is a definite yes, and I'm looking forward to living and working happily in Japan for the long term; possibly even for the rest of my life. Thanks to the support of my many sensei and friends and opportunities to study, learn, improve and maintain my Japanese over the past 20 years, not to mention my own considerable efforts, the key to live and work in Japan, communicate with Japanese, consume Japanese media, and negotiate Japanese culture is in my hand.

Mastering Japanese has truly been the gift that keeps on giving.

AFTERWARD

I hope that you enjoyed this book and that my story has provided you with insight into what it really takes to go beyond rudimentary classroom learning and develop your Japanese to an exceptional level that enables you to become a functionally fluent, literate and culturally informed user of Japanese for whatever goals, purposes or pleasures you may have.

In closing, let me remind you once again that while it certainly is possible to "master" Japanese so that you acquire the "*knowledge and skill that allows you to do, use, or understand something very well,*" when it comes to learning languages in general and Japanese in particular, the journey is as perpetually endless as it is infinitely rewarding.

And Finally

If you enjoyed this book and found it informative and useful, please consider writing a favorable review on Amazon.com to help the book reach a wider audience of aspiring Japanese learners.

For more insight into Japan and the Japanese language from the author, be sure to also check out the **Confessions of a Japanese Linguist Blog** at:

howtomasterjapanese.com